Also by Nora Sayre
    Sixties Going On Seventies

Running Time

Running

Time : FILMS OF THE COLD WAR

Nora Sayre

The Dial Press
New York

Published by
The Dial Press
1 Dag Hammarskjold Plaza
New York, New York 10017

Portions of this book appeared in somewhat different
form in *The Nation*, *Grand Street*, and in *The Progressive*.
Reprinted by permission from *The Nation*,
Nation Associates Incorporated, Copyright © 1978
and 1979.
Reprinted by permission from *The Progressive*,
409 East Main Street, Madison, Wisconsin 53703.
Copyright © 1980, The Progressive, Inc.

Library of Congress Cataloging in Publication Data

Sayre, Nora.
    Running time.

    Bibliography: p.
    Includes index.
    1. Moving-pictures—United States—History.
2. United States—Civilization—1945–   I. Title.
II. Title: Cold War.
PN1993.5.U6S315   791.43′09′09358   81-12637
ISBN 0-385-27621-4   AACR2

For my cousin, Mary Sayre Haverstock,
 and for Lavinia and Frank Monaco and Vivien Asquith

Contents

Acknowledgments

There are so many people who have contributed to this book that my gratitude spans several generations. Some were consulted for a longer and rather different book about the Fifties, but their insights are essential to this one.

A fellowship from the John Simon Guggenheim Foundation and one from the National Endowment for the Arts sustained me throughout the research for this book and another one to come; the fellowships also enabled me to travel for interviews and to rent films, and I am extremely grateful to the providers, as I am to The MacDowell Colony and Yaddo, where parts of both books were written.

Lillian and Phillip Gerard gave me inestimable background and early encouragement, and Elizabeth Faragoh and Philip Dunne guided me to material that I would not have unearthed without their generosity and advice.

Interviews and discussions with the following were invaluable: Larry Adler, James Aronson, Cedric Belfrage, Laslo Benedek, Alvah Bessie, Arthur Birnkrant, Betsy Blair, Patricia Bosworth, Leonard and Jean Boudin, Victor Chapin, Lester Cole, Henry Steele Commager, Sarah Cunningham, Carl Foreman, Frances Goodrich and Albert Hackett, Dorothy Healey, Elia Kazan, Ring Lardner, Jr., Ephraim London, Albert Maltz, Josephine Martin, Arthur Miller, Florence Mischel, Jessica Mitford, Sam Moore, Karen Morley, Abraham and Sylvia Polonsky, Victor Rabinowitz, John Randolph, Maurice Rapf, Sidney Roger, Howard Roller, Budd Schulberg, Nevitt Sanford, Gloria Stuart, Norma Sullivan, Edith Tiger, Robert Treuhaft, and Joseph Wershba. To all of them, my great and special thanks.

I was fortunate to have extensive interviews and conversations with the late Harold Clurman, the late Nunnally Johnson, the late Carey McWilliams, the late Donald Ogden Stewart, the late H. H. Wilson, and the late Ella Winter. My late father, Joel Sayre, shared many of his memories of Hollywood.

I am especially indebted to Peter Meyer of Corinth Films for obtaining the elusive prints of some of the key films examined: thirty of them were screened in the home of Peter Meyer and Gail Niemann; their willingness to live with the images of the Cold War helped to make this book possible, and Mr. Meyer provided indispensable information on many levels.

To Erik Wensberg and James Chace I owe immense and very personal thanks for detailed editorial advice.

Charles Silver, the director of the Film Study Center of the Museum of Modern Art, has been extremely helpful since the beginning, and the Museum's Department of Film has aided me in innumerable ways: I thank Stephen Harvey and his colleagues. The majority of the photographs were furnished by the Film Stills Department of the Museum of Modern Art.

I also thank Linda Amster of *The New York Times*, Eugene Stavis, Emily Sieger of the Library of Congress, Carlos Clarens, Douglas Lemza of Films, Incorporated, and Donald Krim for all their help.

I am very grateful to my agents, Georges and Anne Borchardt, for their counsel and support, and to my editor, Frances McCullough.

Running Time

PRELUDE

This book is the offspring of another; immersed in a vast project concerning many aspects of the Fifties, fascinated by the ways in which the mentalities of the period were reflected on the screen, I wrote a long section on film that overflowed the boundaries of the parent volume, hence it now stands on its own. I was first propelled back to the Fifties by recalling the fears and inhibitions of that era during the final spasms of the Sixties—when it seemed as though the last traces of the Eisenhower years were being expunged, as though we would not re-experience such rigid social constraints, or an ethical equivalent of the Cold War.

Rueful hindsight demands reassessment of even muted optimism. Still, as a student of change and contradiction, I don't believe that we literally repeat ourselves. Instead—because each decade tends to disown or trash its predecessor—there are cycles that resurrect buried themes, which are soon dressed in new garments. But certain images do seem intrinsic to each period, and the emblems of fear that were prevalent in the Fifties were appropriate to the time, when Thoreau's *Walden* was banned in USIA libraries because it was "socialistic," when the Columbia Broadcasting System learned that many viewers really did believe

3

that Edward R. Murrow was a Soviet agent, when the CIA and the army spent millions of dollars on thirteen years of experiments that tested "unwitting" citizens with LSD and psychochemicals— even though a high-level military study group had reported in 1953 that the Russians did not yet excel at mind control and that there was "little threat, if any, to [our] national security"—when some Americans thought that they should shave their dogs and cats to prevent their fur from becoming radioactive.

Meanwhile, those who criticized the prosecution of American Communists, ex-Communists, or independent radicals, discovered that defending the rights of such persons was often thought to be synonymous with condoning the crimes of Stalin. Almost any kind of dissent—especially that which questioned the premises of American society and how it functioned—could be suspected of Communist inspiration. But while public figures discussed the imminence of World War III, those of us who were in school or college were isolated from the central issues, mainly because our teachers were afraid to mention politics in front of us—in or out of the classroom. So we dwelled in a synthetic safety zone—inaccessible to the remnants of the Left or the evangelists of the Right—because the fear in the air had deadened our ability to respond to either one of them.

Those who proclaimed the end of ideology made many feel that social questions or problems no longer existed. (That "ideology" meant socialism wasn't made clear to students, who ingested the notion that all political philosophies were worthless.) We heard that poverty was rare, that equality had nearly been achieved; since the economy was flourishing, many assumed that our society must be healthy. The rhythms of middle-class life seemed to suggest that there was little to protest—except "conformity"—or to explore—except sex; sources of adventure seemed to be sparse. Therefore, for the very young, personal life was paramount; the only commitments would be to love or to art, or to the expansion of the self. Still, the culture kept warning us against "excess": of feeling or involvement. So, even in that realm, few proceeded without a soft pedal; as Warren Miller wrote in *The Way We Live Now*, a novel that evokes the period more pungently for me than any other, "You had only to be careful and not immerse yourself too deep in life, keeping one foot always on dry land for a quick withdrawal when the current got too strong." Living with one dry foot is one of my images of the Fifties, and so is the neatly folded copy of *The New York Times* that lay unread in the common room of my college dormitory each day, and "decorum" as a literary standard, and the Pepsi-Cola douche as a form of birth control.

·

As many have noted, our national memory is meager: if the Fifties and even Vietnam seem as remote as the Peloponnesian wars, it is partly because each American generation neglects to pass on its experience to the next; outside of the university, we don't respect our history, as Europeans do. Our talent is for living in the present: that elation is beguiling during spells of relative calm, but each new crisis sends us reeling—because it seems unprecedented, and because the past itself is suspect: arthritic as well as old.

Seeking an education about the Fifties that I did not receive during that decade, I queried my seniors; quite a few seemed surprised that someone should want to raise the dust from an ugly era. Better forgotten, some said: let it rest. But as I pressured the survivors, a number reacted by first referring to an earlier time: they could not discuss anti-Communism or loyalty oaths or blacklisting without touching on what had led up to them. What follows is a brief summary of some national convulsions—familiar to those who remember Little Rock and the first Sputnik, but included for readers who weren't exposed to the spectacle of Joseph McCarthy frothing and lunging throughout the Army-McCarthy hearings, or the cool restraint of the Modern Jazz Quartet, or the published diagrams of Dwight Eisenhower's heart valves, or campaigns for chlorophyll toothpaste.

·

The middle-class experience of the Thirties—when severe deprivation was flavored with the dread of unending poverty—fueled a confidence in impending change: monumental changes in our society seemed possible because they seemed imperative, and many believed that life would improve—because it had to. Before the New Deal programs were implemented—when even temperate citizens were saying that they would break into bakeries or grocery stores before they would allow their children to starve, when those who were evicted for being unable to pay the rent put their furniture on the street and sat waiting for friends or relatives to take them in—the Left reasoned that socialism was inevitable, and liberals would soon welcome Roosevelt's relief agencies. In short, despite the economic anguish—in part, because of it—the decade was also tinged with hope: that the worst inequities would not remain unaltered. In response to the Depression and the rise of fascism in Europe, a number of Americans became Communists—in spite of all the disagreements among those who thought themselves progressive or enlightened. And, while conservatives railed against the inception of Social Security or the Works Progress Administration, liberals and radicals were not greatly worried by the onslaughts of the Right, because Roosevelt's presence in the White House made them feel more powerful than they were. Although Congressman Martin Dies of Texas, who chaired a Special Committee on Un-American Activities from 1938 to 1944, strove to festoon the New Deal with Communism, members of the Left felt that they could cope rationally with the opposition—until the postwar investigations were under way.

When we entered World War II, there was rich confusion among many Americans about our role in it: some hazily assumed that we were fighting "for democracy" and against dictatorships, while others felt that we were enmeshed only because Pearl Harbor had been attacked. The Right believed that Roosevelt—already responsible for every sin in our society—had "dragged" us into global conflict, while the Left and some liberals thought we were at war with racism as much as fascism: that our mission was to defeat international anti-Semitism as well as Hitler.

For many—to whom foreign affairs were intangible, whose foremost concern was the quality of life in this country—the war was being waged simply so that it might be concluded, so that we could return to prewar normalcy, to an idealized American past, laced with the pleasures of the Twenties. But the longing for peace was complicated by the fact that the wartime industries had finally brought an end to the Depression; due to the influx of jobs and rising salaries, numerous citizens were relishing a novel taste of prosperity—though many predicted that the economy would sag as soon as the war was over, repeating the economic slump that followed World War I. So the prospect of peace did not engender a sense of security, and many wondered if we would cease fighting only to relive the despairs of the Depression. In the meantime, for many civilians, the foe was almost faceless—except on the movie screen; enemies were barbarians who demolished distant landscapes, and the concept of being invaded was as foreign to most Americans as the Normandy coast or the byways of Milan.

The unreality of the war permeated even a small child's existence: loving the new red plastic flashlight strapped to my wrist for air-raid drills (drills meant being given candy in a school basement in midmorning), reveling in fantasies of capturing escaped prisoners of war in the sandy marshes of Cape Cod, I savored wartime life even though my father was a foreign correspondent; the dangers that he encountered were inconceivable, since the adults told us that the Allies were certain to win the war. Bombs and guns were toys, or vice versa; though we heard that the duration would require "sacrifices," they remained as insubstantial as death or weapons. Approving laughter from relatives rose when we made hand puppets with eggshell heads for Hitler and Mussolini: we burlesqued their repulsive accents and then we easily destroyed them; each patriotic playlet climaxed with the villains' skulls shattering against the wall.

War did mean missing people—because they were sent to other countries—but it also meant letters with exciting stamps (therefore stamp collections), new bicycles (to save gasoline), marvelous meals from the victory gardens and sometimes the black market, intriguing objects found among the scrap-metal drives, and being permitted to listen to the radio more than usual. And there was so much food that we groaned when we were exhorted to clean our plates for the sake of the children in England and France—we almost envied them because they didn't have to drink as much milk as we did. But it was suggested that we could help them by growing up to be strong and healthy: strong Americans were going to take care of the Europeans, who would need our guidance. So when Henry Luce stated in his "American Century" *Life* magazine editorial that "the complete opportunity of leadership is *ours*," and eulogized "the vision of America as the principal guarantor of the freedom of the seas, the vision of America as the dynamic leader of world trade," his enthusiasm was reflected even in the emptied plates of overfed children—brimming with beneficence because they had eaten more than they wanted to.

But a childlike view of the war wasn't confined to children: the wickedness of the enemy and the righteousness of our cloudy cause were unquestionable to many who nonetheless resented our embroilment in a European war. Although the issues—such as freeing conquered nations—were nebulous, there was never any doubt of our innate goodness or that we deserved to triumph, just as the celestial war heroes did in films like *So Proudly We Hail* and *Air Force*. Still, Archibald MacLeish, who had been the chief of the Office of Facts and Figures, remarked that our "escapist and delusive" movies contributed to the widespread misunderstandings of the purposes of the war. While some of the Hollywood producers were sincerely committed to combating fascism, propaganda was excellent box office, since war is hardly undramatic. In our movies, morality lost all complexity, especially among nations: virtue was American, evil was German, torture was Japanese, bravery was British. Jews were understood to suffer (overseas), although the history of persecution wasn't really acknowledged, and suffering usually took place offscreen. And, as James Agee complained in *The Nation* in 1943, such pictures as *This Land Is Mine* and *The Moon Is Down* populated the occupied countries with "posturing" figures "spouting" lines like "You cannot keel de speerit off a free pipples"—an evocation that Agee found "indecent." He rebelled against "the already over-ripe vocabulary of democratic claptrap which all but destroys our realization that modest heroism is possible, constant, and implicit in this war."

•

Once the war was won, various expectations clashed. Americans had never been given an indication of what our postwar society was meant to be: there was no blueprint for the immediate future. Many liberals hoped for a resumption of the New Deal, while the Left thought that a revival of the Depression would encourage the public to accept radical leadership. Instead, the voluptuous economic expansion that occurred during the Fifties astounded many who had braced themselves for fierce austerity. But if liberals wished to pick up the threads of the Thirties, so did the conservatives: for them, it seemed essential to eradicate the legacy of the dead Roosevelt, to recapture the White House from those whose prewar commitments to the poor had dismayed many of the comfortable and the rich. Also, conservatives blamed the heritage of the New Deal and the Left for the postwar militancy of many labor unions, whose members were determined to raise the salaries that had been frozen during the war.

Roosevelt's confidence that he could handle Stalin had been shared by few. Aversion to the Soviet Union—later intensified by revulsion at Stalin's liquidations—had been common among our politicians ever since the Russian revolution, and that reflex had been only temporarily subdued during the war, due to the alliance against Hitler and then Japan. The assumption that Russia would soon be our adversary dilated as the large Soviet military presence in Eastern Europe fed fears that a victorious Soviet army was going to sweep through Western Europe—although some Kremlinologists argued that Russia was mainly intent on protecting her borders from invasion and solidifying her "spheres of influence." Many Americans concluded that worldwide revolution was the goal—even though a country that had lost twenty million people was hardly fit to wage a major war. Russia's presumed threat to Western Europe was confirmed in many minds by the tightening of the Soviet grip in Eastern Europe, culminating in the Communist takeover in Czechoslovakia in 1948 and the Berlin blockade of the same year. While it was not irrational to fear Soviet aggression abroad, the illusion that American Communists and radicals and even liberals could damage our country from within soon became a national psychosis.

In 1946, Winston Churchill delivered his legendary "Iron Curtain" speech in Fulton, Missouri, in which he said that Communist parties throughout the world constituted "a growing . . . peril to Christian civilization." In March 1947, the Truman Doctrine was unfurled, whereby we provided economic and military aid to suppress a Communist uprising in Greece and to maintain a right-wing monarchy there, while protecting a conservative government in Turkey against the Russians. In order to convince Congress that intervention in Greece was necessary, Truman was urged by Senator Arthur Vandenberg to "scare hell out of the country." Only ten days after Truman asked Congress for four million dollars on behalf of Greece and Turkey, Truman's federal loyalty program was issued, which resulted in the investigation of the political beliefs and associations of all federal employees; "security risks" were purged from their jobs on fragile evidence of "disloyalty"—in a pattern that would soon be repeated throughout a galaxy of professions, even though the far-flung loyalty programs did not unmask any spies.

Not many voices challenged the loyalty order: already, most guessed that if they protested, the finger might be pointed at them. Thereafter, the gains of the Italian and French Communist parties in their own countries, the defeat of Chiang Kai-shek by the Chinese Communists in 1949, and the arrest and confession of atom spy Klaus Fuchs in England gave further momentum to the investigating committees, as did the timing of the Korean War. A vision of a world split in half, where every country would have to side with the Communists or fight them, was shared by many who never imagined that enmity would one day develop between the Soviet Union and China—and when the two nations diverged in the late Fifties, John Foster Dulles refused to believe it.

Looming throughout the political investigations was the traditional Republican loathing of the New Deal (which Alger Hiss seemed to personify), encouraging the allegation that many New Dealers were Communists or fellow travelers—a device that was zealously employed in the attempts to unseat the Democrats in the elections of 1948 and 1952. (Even before the war was over, Clare Boothe Luce had said that "the Communist Party has gone underground, like termites, into the Democratic Party.") Truman, accused by many Republicans of being "soft on Communism," had said that his loyalty program "should take the smear off the Democratic Party." As the "smear" spread instead of contracting, the Catholic church sustained it, and Cardinal Spellman reproached Truman for "appeasing" the American Communist Party. Catholic leaders often announced that the Communists were going to destroy Christianity and morality: the two were identical in the minds of many Christians. Church attendance had declined right after the war; the Catholics needed a religious crusade, and the heresy hunt helped to unify their church. The Protestants also felt the need of a revival in their own church, and their dignitaries endorsed the creed of anti-Communism.

At the same time, conservative southerners surmised that those who worked for civil rights—known as "agitating the Negroes"—were pro-Soviet. Some of the investigators nourished the idea: Albert Canwell, the chairman of the Washington State Legislative Fact-Finding Committee on Un-American Activities, declared, "If someone insists that there is discrimination against Negroes in this country, or that there is inequality of wealth, there is every reason to believe that person is a Communist." The supposition that whites who upheld racial equality were Bolshevik schemers meshed with some of the emotions that had been roused during the war, concerning the definition of the enemy—and along with the postwar fear of Russia, there emerged a concept of a foe that was as much an internal betrayer as an external threat. Many southern whites felt betrayed by other whites who sought to impose alien practices upon them, such as integrated schools. To some, the specter of the Soviet Union seemed to have entered their own communities: among teachers, within trade unions, even on movie screens—whatever was close to home. Meanwhile, the fear and dislike of the liberal eastern establishment and its universities served to heighten the anti-intellectualism which was always endemic to this country; Harvard and cities and civil libertarians and "all those fags in striped pants who lost China for us" were lumped together as the enemy.

The consternation—even panic—that was generated by the first Soviet atom bomb test in September 1949 mounted in the decade that followed. No country but ours was meant to have atomic or nuclear weapons, and our monopoly was supposed to guarantee peace—on the grounds that they would never be used after Hiroshima. Since nature reveals her secrets only to Americans, it was thought that the Russians would be incapable of inventing such marvels. Some wanted to believe that the bomb had been stolen from us, and the Rosenberg case convinced many that the Russians' espionage had been successful. The Rosenbergs' execution fanned the obsession: when people are sent to jail or put to death, they really do seem dangerous.

Due to the charges leveled against their party, many Democrats thought they had to surpass the Republicans in the war on domestic Communism. While it was logical that moderate liberals should wish to disassociate themselves from the Communists— since the two groups had disagreed so violently and so often— some liberals felt that it was crucial to revile those for whom they feared to be mistaken. Hubert Humphrey proposed a bill that would outlaw the Communist Party, and he supported a plan to send Communists to internment camps—which he regretted when it was too late. The McCarran Internal Security Act, which was passed in 1950, entitled the president to order that "dangerous" Americans be rounded up and imprisoned during "internal security emergencies." The Act also required all Communists and Communist organizations to register with the newly created Subversive Activities Control Board (no one did register, and in 1965 the Supreme Court ruled that registering was equal to self-incrimination). Meanwhile, between 1953 and 1959, the American Civil Liberties Union not only refused to defend Communists, but donated information about some of its own members to the FBI. A few ACLU officials gave the FBI the names of their colleagues who criticized the bureau. And a couple of persons who solicited the ACLU's aid in organizing a campaign against the Committee were also named—by the ACLU to the FBI. It was hoped that friendly relations with the FBI would armor the ACLU against those who labeled it a Communist organization.

In 1952, many mistook Adlai Stevenson's literacy for ultra-liberalism, even though he sometimes went further than the Republicans in chastising the Communists. (Some radicals voted for Eisenhower because they thought that his anti-Communism was less vehement than Stevenson's.) At the start of his first presidential campaign, Stevenson addressed a national convention of the American Legion, identifying Communism as "the strangulation of the individual" and "the death of the soul. Americans who have surrendered to this misbegotten idol have surrendered their right to our trust." But when he added, "We must take care not to burn down the barn to kill the rats," his rivals responded gleefully; Richard Nixon said that Stevenson had "made light of the menace of Communism." Hence the Democratic candidates continued to dwell in a double bind; Stevenson had called Joseph McCarthy's methods "an hysterical, putrid form of slander" and had vetoed several "anti-subversive" bills in Illinois, but he said that Communists should be "excluded" from the educational system, and he praised J. Edgar Hoover's "magnificent, superb" performance in "catching Communist agents like killing poisonous snakes or tigers."

•

A word that will not appear in this book is "McCarthyism"—nor will there be any references to "the McCarthy era": a term which reduces the whole history of anti-Communism to the behavior of one individual. The senator was a by-product and a symbol of the period, not its creator; he merely capitalized on an already fertile movement when he urgently needed a campaign issue. In January 1950, when he was still an obscure figure outside of Wisconsin, he dined with three fellow Catholics to seek advice on a theme for his bid for re-election in 1952; an attorney proposed promoting the St. Lawrence Seaway, and McCarthy also considered developing a new pension plan. Then a priest suggested Communism, and McCarthy seized on the subject that would hurl him into national prominence one month later.

But many still misunderstand the Fifties because they assume that "McCarthyism" died when the man did—or when he lost his colossal personal power. And some who called him "dreadful" really meant that someone else could do a better job, that Mc-Carthy was besmirching the cause of anti-Communism: with the sleaziness of his style, his panoramic lies, and his appetite for abusing the establishment—as when he said that General George Marshall was "always and invariably serving the world power of the Kremlin," or when he called Henry Luce "a debased, de-graded, degenerate liar." Many of McCarthy's critics were in-censed because he molested so many non-Communists, but the civil liberties of Communists were hardly a popular issue.

McCarthy thrived for four years because of his talent for wielding imagery—"One Communist with a razor blade poised over the jugular vein of this nation or in an atomic energy plant can mean the death of America"—and because he gave the impression that the Communists had *already* managed to pervert a part of our society, and especially because politicians feared that he could ruin their careers by turning voters against them. The Hearst papers supported him, as did the McCormick and Scripps-Howard papers, and so did *The Saturday Evening Post* and *U.S. News and World Report*. He was skilled at galvanizing hatred and outrage, particularly among voters who felt they had been dis-dained or ignored by eastern liberals.* For a time he succeeded in paralyzing Truman, and then Eisenhower, by keeping them on the defensive while he savaged many in their administrations. Yet, as Richard Rovere observed, he was neither a totalitarian nor

---

* On February 20, 1950, he read the following into the *Congressional Record*: "It is not the less fortunate or members of the minority groups who have been selling this nation out but rather those who have had all the benefits the wealthiest nation on earth has to offer—the finest homes, the finest college edu-cations, and the finest jobs in the government that we can give. This is glaringly true of the State Department. There the bright young men who were born with silver spoon in their mouth [*sic*] are the ones who have been worse [*sic*]."

"even a reactionary," but a nihilist without any interest in the social order, "a revolutionist without any revolutionary vision." Rovere also described him as "a political speculator, a prospector who drilled Communism and saw it come up a gusher. He liked his gusher, but he would have liked any other just as well."

McCarthy was riding a tide that had swelled long before he learned how to swim in it; antipathy toward radicals and other precursors of the American Communist Party dated back to the early decades of this century—even then, socialism had been regarded as a foreign and therefore ominous import. Postwar anti-Communism was enriched by the attorney general's list, which was assembled in 1947 to facilitate Truman's loyalty program. If federal employees had belonged to any of the seventy-eight "subversive" organizations listed—such as the American Committee for the Protection of the Foreign Born or American Youth for Democracy—they were almost certain to lose their jobs. When the list was published, many who worked outside the government found themselves unemployable—if they had ever signed a petition, gone to a meeting, or contributed money to various anti-fascist groups of the Thirties, some of which had been dominated by the American Communist Party. (The FBI conducted investigations for the list while the bureau was also developing its own lavish files on the loyalty of private citizens, and the FBI and the Committee exchanged material that aimed—in J. Edgar Hoover's words—to "expose, discredit, and disrupt" groups that attacked the Committee.) In 1953, Eisenhower's new loyalty program was even harsher than Truman's, and twenty-two hundred federal employees were discharged in the year of its inception, even though none were proved to be Communists.

Although many Communists of the Thirties had left the Party by 1950, popular mythology wedded their former membership to espionage: during the Cold War, anyone who had ever been a Communist was considered a potential spy for the Soviet Union. It was not widely understood that numerous Communists had first been drawn to the organization because they were gravely concerned about poverty and justice and racism in America. Since the Soviet constitution of 1936 had declared that anti-Semitism was illegal, and because Stalin appeared to be an implacable enemy of the Nazis, some had felt that joining the Party meant working against every kind of racism. Most were quite ignorant of the ideologies that lacerated the Soviet Union: few perceived that the Soviet state was hardly the embodiment of Marxism. But the first socialist country in the world had been their model, the experiment which they so eagerly hoped would succeed—so much emotion was poured into protecting the right of the Soviet Union to survive. Hence, for a while, many had been unable to believe that Stalin had killed millions of his countrymen; they thought that reactionaries were inventing falsehoods about Russia. For some, it had been unimaginable that Communists who had united against the czars could betray or murder one another, or persecute Jews.

Often citing the exposé of *The New York Times*'s wildly distorted accounts of the Russian revolution—written and published in 1920 in *The New Republic* by Walter Lippmann and Charles Merz, who called the *Times*'s reporting "nothing short of a disaster"— the Communists reassured themselves that the American press coverage of the Moscow trials and the Soviet tortures and mass executions was a monstrous fabrication, a conspiracy against the international Left. (Later, many older Communists were devastated to learn that they had been wrong; their juniors, who had joined in the Forties, were less interested in Russian history than in American problems.) But some Communists had invited the wrath of genuine liberals when they defended the Nazi-Soviet Pact to the extent of branding its American opponents as "social fascists" and "turncoats"—and the rapid switch of the Party line after the Germans invaded Russia won them no respect from those who had persistently hated Hitler, who could never forget Stalin's purges. After the war, the Communists' uncritical adherence to the foreign policy of the Soviet Union meant that much of the public would view them as "agents of a foreign power," as traitors dedicated to the decimation of democracy.

•

When the House Committee on Un-American Activities investigated the film industry in October 1947, the goal was publicity—for the Republican Committee members who hoped to help the GOP win the elections of 1948. Committee chairman J. Parnell Thomas, who asserted that Hollywood had become "a Red propaganda center," concentrated on many film makers' allegiance to Roosevelt and deduced that the government had inspired some of the studios to make pro-Soviet movies during the war. In the pattern of the time, it was the Committee's intention to equate the New Deal with Communism, and to persuade the voters that Truman was perpetuating the New Deal (when he was actually retreating from its policies). But even before the hearings of 1947, Thomas seemed to be sure that the Hollywood Communists had inserted their politics into their scripts—though almost no evidence was submitted, and despite the fact that screenwriters had hardly any control over their material after it reached the producers. Some of the Committee members favored government censorship of movies, and William Randolph Hearst had published a signed editorial demanding such restraints. Both conservative producers and radical or liberal film makers worried that federal forces might eventually try to censor the whole communications industry.

But Hollywood's overwhelming attraction for the Committee was its celebrities: the investigators had a fixation on the famous. Although the public hardly knew the names of writers or directors, the word "Hollywood" conferred a kind of royalty—which meant dazzling exposure and banner headlines for the Committee. Also, for Thomas's predecessor, Mississippi Congressman John Rankin, who had reactivated the Committee in 1945, Jews and Communists were barely distinguishable—and much of the power in Hollywood was Jewish. Rankin said in 1945 that those who were plotting to "overthrow the government" had their "headquarters in Hollywood," which was "the greatest hotbed of subversive activities in the United States." And a number of uninformed Americans came to believe him.

The Committee had been beckoned to Hollywood in 1947 by

the Motion Picture Alliance for the Preservation of American Ideals, a passionately anti-Communist organization which had been established in 1944 to vanquish "the growing impression that this industry is made up of, and dominated by, Communists, radicals, and crackpots." The Alliance's Statement of Principles maintained that "co-existence is a myth and neutrality is impossible . . . anyone who is not FIGHTING Communism is HELPING Communism." The group, like the Committee, was initially prone to focus on the content of films, and one of its members said that the Alliance planned "to turn off the faucets which dripped red water into film scripts." The Alliance provided most of the friendly witnesses who testified before the Committee, including Ayn Rand, who was the only ideologue of Hollywood's right wing and therefore an adornment to the Alliance. Meanwhile, the most fervent anti-Communists in Hollywood—like those throughout the country—were also animated by the wave of postwar strikes among many trade unions; right-wingers like Walt Disney were positive that some unions were guided by the Communists. But although Party members were deeply involved in the Hollywood labor movement, they didn't control it, as their antagonists insisted.

The preoccupations of the Cold War sprang to nationwide attention through the prosecution of the Hollywood Ten; in retrospect, many lawyers believe that it raised the largest questions about civil liberties of any case of that era. As the liberal screenwriter Philip Dunne has explained, the Committee's "hearings" were really "extra-legal trials in which the accused were denied normal constitutional safeguards, in which the prosecutor's witnesses could not be cross-examined, and in which the Committee itself acted as prosecutor, judge, and jury." The Hollywood Ten was the first group of American Communists to be punished by the engine of postwar conservatism, which depicted Communists as dangerous revolutionaries and successful spies—neither of which had ever existed in Hollywood. The Committee justified its course by stating that it was holding hearings for the purpose of enacting legislation that would deal with the Communist threat.

When the defendants—Alvah Bessie, Herbert Biberman, Lester Cole, Edward Dmytryk, Ring Lardner, Jr., John Howard Lawson, Albert Maltz, Samuel Ornitz, Adrian Scott, and Dalton Trumbo—were asked by the Committee if they were or ever had been Communists, all of them took the First Amendment; by doing so, some hoped to make a political statement: declaring that the First Amendment forbade Congress to pass any law that could curtail the freedom of speech or opinion, and that therefore the government had no right to investigate a citizen's beliefs. (In that interpretation, the First guarantees the right to remain silent as well as the right to speak.) The Committee for the First Amendment, a group of liberal professionals organized by Philip Dunne, John Huston, and William Wyler to oppose the procedures of the Committee and to forestall censorship and blacklisting, argued that "any investigation into the political beliefs of the individual is contrary to the basic principles of our democracy. Any attempt to curb freedom of expression and to set arbitrary standards of Americanism is in itself disloyal to both the spirit and the letter of the Constitution."

Throughout the Fifties, some lawyers who had radical clients debated the choice between the First and the Fifth Amendments; the First was considered preferable, since it challenged the legality of the existence of the Committee and defended the tradition of free speech in this country. The Fifth—which affirmed that no one could be "compelled in any criminal case to be a witness against himself"—merely shielded the individual against self-incrimination: a stance that tainted him as well, since it suggested that he harbored a guilty secret. But some of the Communist film makers were proud of their political past, and they did not want their anti-fascist activities to be classified as "criminal." In the end, the fate of the Hollywood Ten demonstrated that taking the First usually resulted in a jail sentence for contempt of Congress, or in years of very expensive litigation, while the Fifth did keep many out of prison—although they lost their jobs because the Committee had succeeded in depriving the Fifth of its legitimacy, and most Americans believed that anyone who invoked the Fifth was a Communist.

The Left at first expected that the Hollywood Ten would win their case. While the Ten knew that they would be cited for contempt—for refusing to confirm or deny Party membership—and that they would lose in the trial court and the appellate court, and that they all risked a year in jail, they thought that they would be vindicated in the Supreme Court. By contesting the power of the Committee to legislate in the field of political associations, they hoped to destroy it in the courts, to rid the country of the political inquisitions. Their lawyers anticipated a five-to-four ruling, and they moved to postpone the case until after the 1948 elections, reasoning that the Supreme Court would be affected if Henry Wallace did well: if he received five to seven million votes. (He got slightly over one million.) But the two most liberal members of the Court, Frank Murphy and Wiley B. Rutledge, died in the summer of 1949, before the second round of hearings—and that changed the composition of the Court, which turned down the Ten's petition to be heard. In 1950, they all went to jail.

It was characteristic of the period that the legal position of the defendants was thoroughly misunderstood by many Americans. Their detractors—including many liberals—thought that people who were or had been Communists should say so on the witness stand. But many observers didn't realize that those who admitted that they had belonged to the Party would then have to give the names of other Communists, or to go to prison for contempt: there was no other option. A few of the Ten wished to say that they were Communists. But if someone conceded membership, he then lost the legal right to remain silent and would be asked to inform on others, a role that was unacceptable to many—although not to Edward Dmytryk, who recanted after a few months in jail; in 1951, he gave twenty-six names to the Committee. A witness who named others could be fairly sure of returning to work at the studios; in order to be re-employed, he had to identify persons who would be fired as a result of his testimony—his future livelihood would cost them theirs.

Toward the end of the 1947 investigations, J. Parnell Thomas promised that the Committee would produce "an extensive study" of Communist propaganda in motion pictures, but that document never appeared. Throughout the 1951–1952 hearings—in which the Committee assaulted the film industry with more ferocity than ever—the content of movies was of far less consequence than the naming of names, and of course the Committee was still more interested in publicity than in political heresies: this time, many of the hearings were televised. Nearly a third of the witnesses became informers; although the Committee and the FBI already knew the names that were provided, the ritual of public repentance was supposed to be a test of the witness's sincerity. His repudiation of Communism also helped to advertise the potency of the investigators.

The Committee—chaired by John S. Wood after J. Parnell Thomas had been imprisoned for payroll padding—was further stimulated by the knowledge that the Hollywood Left had raised considerable funds for particular causes, such as ambulances for the Spanish Loyalists, or refugees from fascist countries, or the more radical unions. The inquisitors were aware that the gifts to some front groups had benefited the American Communist Party, until blacklisting erased the salaries of the most affluent contributors. Meanwhile, although film content had waned as a pivotal issue, some Americans had been induced to think that our movies were seething with Communist doctrine.

·

In 1947, few on the Left had foreseen that members of the Committee would tell producers like Jack Warner that the studios should rid themselves of "termites," and many had accepted the assurances of Eric Johnston, the president of the Motion Picture Association, that there would never be a blacklist. But the producers soon reversed that decision, and the Screen Writers Guild was instructed that no writer who was thought to be a Communist could be hired. As the blacklist lengthened in the early Fifties, there was also a graylist: non-Communists who had radical associations weren't often fired outright, but they were moved to innocuous positions and barred from promotion, and many had great difficulties in finding new jobs. Throughout, it was perilous to be a civil libertarian: protesting blacklisting could be interpreted as supporting the Communist Party.

By briskly firing those who had participated in the politics of the Left, the studios collaborated with the Committee because they were terrified that the charges of Communism could wreck their industry, which was already losing its audience to television. If the name of any suspect appeared on a screen credit, the American Legion and kindred right-wing groups might picket their next movies; hence financiers would not wish to invest in them, distributors would not want to handle them, and most projectionists would refuse to run them. The power of the Legion was formidable: with almost three million members and many auxiliaries, the Legionnaires could rally support in communities all over the country; they wrote letters, sent telegrams, and telephoned studios, networks, and sponsors about the political affiliations of many entertainers.

The producers feared that millions would shun the films that the Legion condemned, since it would be un-American to cross that picket line. The Legion's demonstrations outside movie houses exhibiting Charlie Chaplin's *Monsieur Verdoux* resulted in the movie being withdrawn from circulation, and the Legion and the Catholic War Veterans succeeded in dissuading many theater owners and some television stations from reviving Chaplin's silent films. The Fox West Coast Theatres and Loew's Theatre Circuit canceled Chaplin's *Limelight* when the Legion vowed to picket. The stage version of *Death of a Salesman* was closed in Cairo, Illinois after the Legion picketed it there; the Legionnaires were infuriated not only by Arthur Miller's opposition to the Committee, but by the subject of the play, which they described as "a time bomb under American business." Neither Chaplin nor Miller had ever been a Communist, nor had John Huston nor José Ferrer, whose *Moulin Rouge* was picketed by the Legion until the director and the star met with one of its officers, who said that both had "indicated that they will go all the way with us in fighting Communism." And the Catholic War Veterans picketed *Born Yesterday* and *The Marrying Kind*, distributing leaflets that called Judy

Holliday "the darling of *The Daily Worker*," until the actress confirmed her guilelessness before the Senate Internal Security Subcommittee.

While the Committee and the FBI usually knew who had belonged to the Communist Party, the fantasies spread by the watchdogs of patriotism and free-lance informers were frequently accepted as "evidence" against those who were under scrutiny. After the 1951 hearings, the Legion's leadership expressed angry doubts that the studios had expelled a sufficient number of left-wingers, and their vigilance increased. Studio officials promised the Legion not to hire anyone who took the Fifth Amendment, and asked the Legion for its own files on suspects. The "loyalty" of the employees of all the major studios was checked against the Legion's carelessly compiled dossiers, which could jeopardize someone's job if he or she had attended a benefit for Russian war relief, or a rally for the Hollywood Ten, or signed a statement criticizing the Committee.

And the firing of individuals in every profession—from teachers to salesmen and linotypers and union leaders and librarians—recurred so that their employers could proclaim their unsullied Americanism. Hopes that the Supreme Court would rule blacklisting illegal were defunct by 1951, when the practice accelerated. In the meantime, Roy Brewer, the chairman of the Motion Picture Alliance for the Preservation of American Ideals and the leader of the International Alliance of Theatrical Stage Employees, which dominated film labor circles, had helped to refine the clearance industry—that is, he negotiated the confessions and rehabilitations of ex-Communists and some liberals who regretted their previous associations. Brewer steered them to the FBI to contribute their "information" about Communists, and then to the Committee. By 1952, Brewer and a few others in the Alliance, like Hedda Hopper, along with the Legion and such columnists as George Sokolsky and Victor Riesel, acquired the power to determine who could—or could not—be employed by the studios: they were regarded as authorities on political purity, and producers were afraid to hire anyone of whom they did not approve.

In Hollywood, the reasons offered for refusing to hire the undesirables were nonpolitical: actors were informed that they were too short or too tall, too old, "not the right type" for a given role. Since they couldn't work under pseudonyms, as writers did, some actors lost at least fifteen years out of their working lives—for many, the movie blacklist lasted until 1965. And writers were quite often told that being discharged or having their scripts rejected had nothing to do with their politics—that they just weren't writing well. Naturally, those who were notified that their talents were dwindling sometimes came to feel that it was true: they could no longer feel confident of their calling. An actor who knew that the studios didn't dare to cast him would wonder if, after all, he was a mediocre performer. Directors and writers wrestled with work blocks and the debilitations of self-doubt. A screenwriter and novelist who'd enjoyed years of success became dubious of what he produced after he was blacklisted; remembering how demoralized he'd been, he drew on an image from baseball: "As pitchers say, I lost my rhythm."

•

It is not my intention here to record the experiences of the blacklisted—that will be part of a subsequent book. I've known quite a few of them, and I know a good deal about the humiliations, the harassments by the FBI, the ravaged family relationships, the health crises and financial emergencies that beset many of them until the mid-Sixties—and about careers that were permanently destroyed. Being fired held a particular horror for those who had come through the Depression, when a job was the most important aspect of a person's life, when losing a job was the worst thing that could happen to anyone. And writing under false names for minimal pay and no credit was deeply demeaning to seasoned professionals who had been proud of their work. As I listened to their histories, I felt it was time to re-examine the movies that had been used as weapons against them, and also to see how the social climate had affected the ensuing chapters of American film making. It was then necessary to go back to some of the movies that Hollywood had produced just before the investigations—as well as those that were made in the years when fear governed even the inscape of entertainment, just as it ruled the conduct of our schools and universities and the Senate and the Congress.

The apolitical aspects of the Fifties interest me just as much as the political fervors—and I think that they are equally important. Again, I remember my teachers: some taught us (by their silence) that it was hazardous to possess any politics at all; others— saturated in the New Criticism—seemed to imply that history itself was not significant, that a poem or a novel or a play should be read "apart from its time," detached from its era. Hence, perhaps, my own temptation to relate movies to their temporal backdrops— there is always a pleasure in breaking one's training—but the aesthetics of film absorb me as much as history does.

A seventeen-year-old recently asked me: Do movies change, or do we? And if some of our early favorites now seem tepid or witless, or if certain B-pictures have attained a new luster, we're forced to inspect the cultural luggage that accompanies them—and to review our own vicissitudes as well. For this book, I watched the films of the Fifties from the perspective of the late Seventies, acknowledging that our perceptions are salted with contemporary consciousness, aware that the late Sixties atomized both the inhibitions and the placidities of the Fifties. The task was twofold: to see the movies in the context of the time, and to measure them against the insights that we've acquired—or the quandaries that have besieged us—since they were released.

When we saturate ourselves in old films, we can employ them as hidden memories of a decade—directly or indirectly, they summon up the nightmares and daydreams that drifted through segments of our society—and exploring them from a distance unearths many of the obsessions of the past. One theme that does emerge from some of the movies of the Fifties is the uncertainty about the nature or the location of our enemies: the Communist who operates behind the scenes, the delinquents who lurk around the next corner, the prehistoric monsters reactivated by the atom tests of science fiction, or the neighbors whose brains are manipulated by Martian technology, seem to be part of a vast mosaic of ambiguous fears. What was threatening was right in our midst—the subversive who belonged to the Parent-Teachers' Association or the dinosaur that reared up in one's backyard—and many movies emphasized that the peril was ubiquitous: arresting a few "Marxist leaders" or vanquishing some titanic insects was only a temporary solution, since the creatures were adept at reproducing themselves with appalling speed.

In the years when we had little communication with our perceived enemy, the Soviet Union, the movies also stressed a dread of the unknown: the Martians or the wandering social outcasts who disrupted communities for no comprehensible purpose. Extraterrestrials and Communists spied on innocent American citizens, black leather jackets followed them down dark alleys, but the outlines of the assailants weren't as pronounced as those of the Nazi or Japanese villains of wartime movies. Meanwhile, as some films featured the struggles that many Americans underwent when they tried to communicate with their own families, the dislocations could be so profound that a housewife might not know if her husband was a drug addict or a fellow traveler or the father of an illegitimate child, and a man could be ignorant that his son was in trouble with the law. In the movies, analyzing personal afflictions appeared to be so arduous that generations and spouses became almost as bewildering to one another as the sense of the larger menace that protracted the Cold War.

Re-entering an historical period through its movies is an experience worth sharing: sometimes, an audience's astonished laughter, or the spectators' small sounds of disbelief, reveal how radically our attitudes toward heroism or the races or the sexes have altered. Yet we shouldn't permit our esteem for particular films or performances to be diminished because we can't agree with what they express—to do so would blind us to the magnificence of *The Triumph of the Will,* or the charms of some "women's pictures," or the emotional impact of *On the Waterfront.* Moreover, it's a mistake to overinterpret Hollywood's "motives": the studios always aimed for recreation and profit, and American films were never financed for love—whatever the aspirations of a director or a writer. The industry merely pined to please: to give the public what it was thought to want, even if the style or content were classed as controversial. But movie-making was and is a random business; although the producers of the Fifties made anti-Communist films to demonstrate that Hollywood was not unpatriotic, the outcome was hardly dictated by a ministry of culture.

Although today we instantly notice the absence of women on the jury in *Twelve Angry Men,* or that the psychiatrist in *The Three Faces of Eve* seems to need a crash course in elemental disorders, or that marriage was a cure for incompatibility, few of the premises were questioned at the time. But as movies age, the more characteristic of their era they become. It's quite easy to perceive the difference between the stated purpose of a film and the unintended results, from the happy endings that now seem forlorn to the somber melodramas that appear as unbridled comedies. Old movies can also set off a chain of very free associations, due to the month or even the day when one saw them: for me, *The Trouble with Harry* triggers the recollection of Autherine Lucy being expelled from the University of Alabama—as the first and only black student there, she was dismissed after riots flared across the campus— and I went to *Rebel Without a Cause* with a pregnant, unmarried friend who had no clues about how to obtain an abortion, and I saw *Somebody Up There Likes Me* during the week when some thought that the Suez crisis might lead to a widening war in the Middle East. Hence movies remind us that we live with cycles, that progress or calamity can be fluid.

.

Commercial films that have waxed in reputation—such as *Pickup on South Street* or *The Barefoot Contessa*—were rarely appreciated for their resonances then. Educated movie-goers were far more snobbish about Hollywood than they are at present; while some sophisticates attended mass market pictures for diversion, their approach was condescending: contemporary American films weren't viewed in the same spirit that was brought to revivals of Chaplin

or Lubitsch, or movies directed by Rossellini or Kurosawa or Buñ-
uel. And while A *Place in the Sun* or *Bad Day at Black Rock* or
Baby Doll can't and shouldn't be measured against *Miss Julie* or
Ugetsu or *La Strada*, we've been liberated from the either/or position that quite sternly divorced American movies from works of
art. Among the erudite critics, James Agee and Manny Farber
were the admirable exceptions, but much of the postwar intelli-
gentsia was grimly suspicious of popular culture: vulgarity was all
that they expected of Hollywood. And even the young—including
devotees of the dreadful—hardly bothered to note distinctions between the amiable nonsense of *The Perfect Furlough* or the lumbering pretensions of *The Goddess* and the eloquent starkness of
Ace in the Hole, because the act of going to the movies was supposed to be lighthearted. Students expected a film to be distract-
ing—to offer relief from concentration—and not many had yet
learned to concentrate on the movie itself.

Prior to the late Forties, movies had given little attention to
the interior life of the young: although Mickey Rooney reappeared
in the *Andy Hardy* cycle, no one was trying to penetrate Andy
Hardy's psyche. But when the film industry discovered that there
was a youth culture and an effort was made to understand its tur-
bulence, most of the actors involved were overage: such mature
performers as Montgomery Clift and Marlon Brando and Paul
Newman were hailed as symbols of rebellion, and death preserved
James Dean's adolescence at the age of twenty-four—while parents
tried to grasp what was meant by alienation. Despite the conservative values of the decade, many of the screenplays were sympathetic to the angry offspring—perhaps because the escalation of
psychiatric treatment in the late Forties and early Fifties had
turned a spotlight on troubled family relationships, and also because the fledglings' revolt was far more dramatic than their elders'
laments.

It was never my ambition to range through all of the key
movies of the Cold War and the Eisenhower years, and I've by-
passed some directors who transcend any period, such as Fritz
Lang and John Ford. And surveys have never seduced me. In-

stead, I selected the films that seemed to me to convey a time when *Ferdinand the Bull* was denounced as left-wing propaganda because the bull refused to fight the matador, when those who failed to embrace the status quo were often called unhealthy, when boned girdles seemed mandatory for very young women, when anxieties about fallout near an atomic testing site in Nevada were dismissed by a local senator as "Communist-inspired scare stories" even after small children began to die of leukemia, when everything evil was somehow imported from Moscow. Since it was also a time when fictions and delusions were accepted as facts, some of the movies may be almost as informative as the FBI's files—and probably more accurate about the mentalities of many Americans who were amused or repelled or touched or unnerved by what they saw on the screen.

1: *Recoiling from Liberalism*

The radiant Slavic faces glowing above embroidered blouses in *Song of Russia* (1944)—in a land where "It's a privilege to drive a tractor"—and the benign chuckles of Stalin in *Mission to Moscow* (1943) were replaced by the grimaces of *The Iron Curtain* (1948), where being Russian means scowling, and by the vast octopus with a moustache snaking its tentacles over a map of the world in *The Red Menace* (1949), when the fervid patriotism of our wartime movies yielded to the Cold War cinema—soon after the House Committee on Un-American Activities began to investigate the film industry.

Before Pearl Harbor, abortive raids had been made on Hollywood by Congressman Martin Dies and the isolationist Senator Burton K. Wheeler. But their efforts were derided when Dies expressed an interest in the ideologies of such persons as Humphrey Bogart and when Wheeler's subcommittee claimed in 1941 that movies like *Sergeant York*—in which Gary Cooper played a hero of World War I—were part of a New Deal plot to involve America in a foreign war. In 1947, the Committee members kept their attention on wartime and postwar films: the movies of the Thirties offered them little ammunition. During the Depression, the Hollywood Left had devoted most of its energies to political organiz-

31

ing—on behalf of the Hollywood Anti-Nazi League and the Committee for the Aid of the Spanish People and certain trade unions. Although some radicals had written extensively for the stage, buoyed by their confidence in "the revolutionary theater," only a few of the Communist screenwriters considered movies to be socially relevant. In the Thirties, there were some, but not many, films about "progressive" subjects, such as *I Am a Fugitive from a Chain Gang*. But these were largely the work of apolitical film makers who were responding to the pressures of the period, when businessmen or landlords often appeared as villains who conspired against blameless citizens—even in the movies of a conservative like Frank Capra. Some radicals were slightly chagrined because *The Grapes of Wrath* was directed by the equally conservative John Ford. But the Left began to search for ways to quicken the social awareness of a mass audience in the late Thirties. And a wave of anti-fascist pictures went into production right after Pearl Harbor was bombed: Communists, liberals, and radicals could and did collaborate throughout the war effort.

Immediately after World War II, some producers were cordial to films that explored current social questions: with an eye on the best-selling books, they correctly sensed that the topical would be profitable. Therefore, until late in 1947, the screenwriters of the Left—including a few of the successful socialist realist playwrights of the Thirties such as Clifford Odets and John Howard Lawson—were able to incorporate some mild versions of their views into their scripts. Still, the opportunities were limited, because the studio executives felt that the public was wary of "messages," and because writers weren't in charge of content: the producers were totally in control of the final screenplays.

Hence even writers who were Communists knew that it was impossible to make left-wing films; still, some were elated by the idea of writing egalitarian material that would be seen by a large public. But at most, they could advance realism and "democratic" themes: they wrote pictures that upheld equality and peace or opposed oppression—in a tone that was tailored to the realities of the movie business, where entertainment and excitement were the perennial priorities. So the aims of the Left were usually modest: to portray an intelligent black character or the erosions of unemployment, or even (although rarely) a woman who earned her own living. Some conveyed sympathy for the labor movement, others depicted the bravery of those who battled fascism abroad; now and then, they were able to eliminate some anti-Soviet implications from a few scenarios. Occasionally, one of the Marxists wrote a script that seemed to condemn the American way of life or the corruptions of our government, but they were revised by the producers to deflect any controversy. However, very few films were as radical as *Body and Soul* (written by Abraham Polonsky and directed by Robert Rossen) or Polonsky's *Force of Evil*, which dissected the consequences of craving much more money than one needs—in a society that encourages the appetite for opulence. Before he was blacklisted, Polonsky wrote brilliantly pessimistic mov ies that were charged with sufficient violence to appeal to popular tastes, and they were concerned with working people—at a time when Hollywood concentrated on the middle class.

Movies about contemporary problems were just beginning to be produced before they became suspect. Since the cycle was extremely successful, Hollywood had started to examine racism, which was thought to be very daring. For over a decade, almost no film had even admitted that a character was Jewish. In the early Thirties, the Anti-Defamation League of B'nai B'rith had persuaded the Jewish producers to stop using Jewish comedians in ethnic roles; with the ascendance of Hitler, it was felt that jokes

(OVERLEAF) Force of Evil, *directed by Abraham Polonsky and co-written with Ira Wolfert in 1948, from Wolfert's novel,* Tucker's People. *The acquisitive characters that Polonsky explored aren't merely greedy: raised in poverty, they have a legitimate hatred of its corrosions. But, in pursuit of cash, they collaborate with criminals who are metaphors for capitalists; self-deception results in self-destruction as the protagonists try to free themselves from the traps that they willingly entered. Here, Thomas Gomez and John Garfield as embattled brothers who can no longer separate themselves from gangsters.*

about being Jewish smacked of anti-Semitism, and a profitable series called *The Cohens and the Kellys* was discontinued. Many Jewish comics—who had thrived in vaudeville—never worked in movies again, since most of the parts that were available to apparent Jews were humorous. The unemployed actors pleaded for other roles—to be allowed to play serious characters—but unless they could be cast as Greeks or Italians or Transylvanians, their film careers died in the Thirties. (The Marx Brothers, Eddie Cantor, and Jack Benny had not been identified with stereotypes, hence they were more fortunate.) Convinced by the Anti-Defamation League that Jews should be neither amusing nor ostentatious, and that it was wise for them to maintain a low profile while Hitler was in power, the producers shunned the issue altogether. But their attitudes changed after the war, when the facts about the Holocaust were known to millions and support for Israel was expanding. By then, many Americans had realized that anti-Semitism was not confined to Germany.

•

In 1947, RKO hastened the completion of *Crossfire* four months before the release of the much more expensive and ambitious *Gentleman's Agreement*. Directed by Edward Dmytryk and produced by Adrian Scott—who would soon become two of the Hollywood Ten—*Crossfire* evokes anti-Semitism far more thoughtfully than its famous competitor. (The novel by Richard Brooks, on which *Crossfire* was based, centered on the murder of a homosexual, who was changed to a Jew for the film.) Constructed as a detective story, the movie skillfully imparts the postwar mood of those who were still searching for an identifiable enemy, plus the habits of hatred encouraged in wartime—a civilian says, "You can *feel* the tension in the air. A whole lot of fight and hate that doesn't know where to go"—and the casual assumption that there will be another war. There's some of the Forties psychology that trickled through the movies of the period, especially when it's repeated that the army can make men hate themselves: for fighting too well—or not well enough. A long speech delivered by a district attorney asserts that racism has murdered Irish Catholics, Jews, Protestants, and Quakers, but carefully omits any reference to black people. The movie hints that decent Americans aren't aware if others are Jewish, and that it's nicer not to notice that anyone belongs to a particular race.

The novel has more fiber than the movie: packed with anti-war themes, it dwells on white hatred of blacks as well as on anti-Semitism, and also on the hostility of heterosexuals toward gay men. In the movie, the only anti-Semite is crazed, and it's implied that he's a rarity. But given *Crossfire*'s limitations, this taut, modest film owes much of its quality to the performances of the three Roberts: Ryan and Mitchum and Young. The latter's pensive weariness as the D.A. highlights the energies of the other two, and Gloria Grahame displays a fine truculence which enlivens her traditional sluttish role. The youthful Mitchum is insolent and sleek; equally cynical about the war and the army and the home front, he's the kind of likable tough who often appears in this species of hardboiled liberal melodrama. Ryan achieves a harsh yet subtle portrait of a racist who's also a traditional reactionary: as an ex-policeman, he's deferential to authority, and his genial moments underline the violence that flares up within him despite his efforts to disguise it. Even as a silent presence, he's all ominous potential: this man can, does, and will kill again. Throughout, the word "stinking" recurs with the savagery of an old-fashioned obscenity—it conveys the fury of the racist in a way that was new to the screen.

Such films, although favorably reviewed, were still thought controversial, and *Gentleman's Agreement* was accused of "Red ideology" by one of Hollywood's anti-Communist pamphleteers. Several Catholic groups also objected to the movie because the heroine was a divorced woman. And some of the prominent Jews in Hollywood protested that *Gentleman's Agreement* should not be filmed at all.

The movie of Laura Z. Hobson's best seller seems ludicrous today, mainly because of the ineptness of the script by Moss Hart. Of course the intentions—to expose the buried anti-Semitism of

liberals—can't be faulted. But the conclusion is disturbing: *Gentleman's Agreement* suggests that if only people wouldn't *behave* badly, or use rude words, then "prejudice" could be eliminated—if everyone could learn good manners, there would be no problem. The movie doesn't deal with the roots of racism, or the passions involved—as *Crossfire* does. It's also stated that there's "no difference" among Americans; according to the film, there's no such thing as racial history or experience or identity. And while it's admitted that jobs or apartments may be denied to those with Jewish surnames, their fiercest punishment appears to be rejection at lush hotels or country clubs.

Gregory Peck, who works for a magazine that seems to be a soft-centered *Time* with some kinship to *Collier's* and *The Saturday Evening Post*, has to embody the dilemmas of writers. (His crusading employer has some lines that enhance his profession. I would cherish an editor who said, "Now get good and comfortable" before revealing that he's "had an idea.") Asked to produce some articles on "bigotry"—"Break it wide open!"—Peck glumly searches for "an angle." Pacing before the typewriter, he rubs the back of his neck, wonders if he's losing his "grip," rolls up his sleeves, loosens his tie, consults his mother—"There isn't any way you can tear open the secret heart of a human being, is there, Ma?"—until the solution finally overwhelms him: "I've got it! The idea, the lead, the angle! It's the only way . . . I'll *be* Jewish!" Humbly, he utters the quintessential writer's line: "The click just happened inside of me." Intent on shaking the dust off anti-Semitism, Peck invariably knits his eyebrows when he says, "Just because I'm Jewish myself. . . ." But his romance with Dorothy McGuire curdles rapidly because—as far as she's concerned—his sham-Jewishness is almost as bad as the genuine article: she reacts as if he had syphilis.

Accelerating in his identification with his role, Peck is told by his Jewish friend John Garfield that he's "telescoping a lifetime"

←

Robert Ryan as the psychotic racist in Crossfire.

into a few weeks, which "makes it hurt more": the dialogue implies that Peck is suffering more than a real Jew would. His small son (Dean Stockwell) is burdened with all the awful questions: frowning at his breakfast cereal, the child asks, "What *are* Jews, anyhow?" and "Say, Pop, are we Jewish?" Outraged by a hotel manager's rebuff at an Adirondacks resort, Peck strides out of the lobby before he's told to sleep in the manger, and soon his fiancée seems to be blaming the entire Jewish race for undermining their relationship.

After his pieces are published, an admiring colleague of Peck's exclaims, "If only everyone would act it out, just one day a year, it'd be curtains overnight!"—thereby giving us the formula for abolishing anti-Semitism. All in all, *Gentleman's Agreement* is worthy of Ring Lardner, Jr.'s response after he first saw it screened: that the movie's moral is that you should never be mean to a Jew, because he might turn out to be a gentile.

•

Five years earlier, Lardner and Michael Kanin wrote *Woman of the Year*: in one scene, Katharine Hepburn—as a Dorothy Thompson figure—spoke a number of languages, including Yiddish. Louis B. Mayer—who kept a silver-framed photograph of Cardinal Spellman in his office—found that distasteful, so another language had to be substituted. Lardner deduced that Mayer felt that making Hepburn speak Yiddish might be interpreted as an attempt by the Hollywood Jews to legitimize themselves—which would be considered "pushy." The Jewish producers continued to be squeamish about this matter—Harry Cohn was even reluctant to contribute to the industry's annual fundraising campaign for Jewish causes—although, as James Agee wrote about the racial films, "Few things pay off better in prestige and hard cash . . . than safe fearlessness."

→

Afflicted with writer's block, Gregory Peck struggles with the complexities of analyzing anti-Semitism in Gentleman's Agreement.

Horrors!
Unbuttoned button-down collar

Samuel Goldwyn later hired Lardner to adapt a book about anti-Semitism in Montreal, titled *Earth and High Heaven*, which Goldwyn had bought at the instigation of his wife. After reading the first draft of the script, Goldwyn said that Lardner had "defrauded and betrayed" him. The producer explained that "just one" of the reasons that he had employed Lardner for the job was because he was a gentile: "You have betrayed me by writing like a Jew." Lardner rewrote the material, and then six other writers worked on it, but none of the screenplays succeeded with Goldwyn. Yet when *Gentleman's Agreement* reached the screen, Goldwyn said that Darryl Zanuck had stolen his idea.

Crossfire had flourished at the box office even after Dmytryk and Scott were blacklisted; *Gentleman's Agreement* was even more lucrative, and won three Oscars. In hopes of a duplicate success, Zanuck commissioned John Ford to direct *Pinky*, which became the second highest earner of 1949. But Ford clashed with Ethel Waters, and Zanuck said later that "Ford's Negroes were like Aunt Jemima. Caricatures." Stricken with shingles, Ford was retired from the movie after ten days' shooting, and Zanuck summoned Elia Kazan, who had also directed *Gentleman's Agreement*. Kazan reshot Ford's footage. Twenty years later, Kazan stressed that neither movie was really his own—although he didn't disown them. Still, he did not choose the casts, and it's almost impossible to detect traces of his style in either film.

In *Pinky*, Jeanne Crain plays a black woman who passed for white in the North; she returns to the impoverished southern town of her childhood to confront "her people." Persistently, the white actress behaves like a princess among peasants. She peers at her black colleagues as though they were exotic animals on display, and her performance seems to ask for our sympathy because she is trapped in this movie. And yet the role brought her the best reviews of her career.

The film seems less concerned with how whites abuse blacks than how badly white trash dares to treat Jeanne Crain, who alternates the lowered lids of shame with being petulant and rueful, or gazing bitterly into space, or arching her back in distress. As her grandmother, Ethel Waters keeps chatting freely with God, also casting her eyes up to heaven, while Crain raises hers to the ceiling: perhaps rolling eyeballs were intended as a sign of negritude. Sometimes she fingers her blouse in gloom. When her white suitor learns that she's "colored," he too stares at the horizon, clutching his jacket in his hands: both performers tend to express intense emotions by pawing their own clothes. Introduced to Waters, he says "How do you do?" as if he were addressing a large plant from another planet. Ethel Barrymore—churlish and bedridden as usual—dies and leaves her property to Crain, which suggests that virtue will thrive if the poor can manage to live next door to the rich and to see them often.

The courtroom scenes where the Barrymore will is contested do have moments that evoke Kazan: the wet southern heat is palpable as the spectators fan themselves and tempers soar with the temperature. At the end, we see the victorious Crain posed before the Barrymore manor house—now a clinic for black nurses—and it's possible to be suddenly touched for the first time in this astounding movie.

The Daily Worker reproached the film for not supporting "inter-racial marriage." Actually, the Motion Picture Code forbade such nuptials until 1956, and a black was not allowed to embrace a white on the screen until 1957. Although Pinky turns down her would-be husband because they "wouldn't be happy together," few women in the audience would find him tempting, so the sacrifice seems small. The sexuality of the film is tame even by the standards of the Forties, but a couple of enthusiastic kisses exchanged between Crain and William Lundigan inspired objections in the South—as did a scene in which two white louts assault Crain after discovering that she's "a dinge." Zanuck's office received some five hundred hate letters about *Pinky*, and when the movie opened at the Rivoli Theater in Manhattan, the manager feared that the large black audiences that journeyed down from Harlem would drive his white clientele away. The manager of the Paramount Theatre in Marshall, Texas, was jailed and fined two hundred dollars for showing *Pinky* for three days—after the city's board of censors had ruled against it. The case went all the way to the Supreme Court, which overturned the censors' ordinance.

However, *Home of the Brave*, produced by Stanley Kramer in 1949, did very well in the South. The film, adapted from Arthur Laurents's play, diminishes the jagged emotional power of the original, partly because the Jewish soldier who's temporarily traumatized by racism in the army becomes a black man in the movie, where he has to be braver than anyone else—which his Jewish counterpart was not. He was also a fine student and a star athlete in high school: in order to plead for equality, the movie makes its one black a superior being. Mark Robson directed the cast to overplay and overreact to a pitch that vitiates the strength of the material, as when the white soldiers gape and freeze at the blackness of a fellow volunteer. In the play, the crude racism of the soldiers was convincing; in the movie, it's so extreme that the seriousness of the theme is diluted. James Edwards, as the black, was made to be far too neurotic, even for a psychiatric case; when he's offended, his nostrils flare and his whole body twitches. Hence the hysteria of the victim makes him seem downright psychotic in his response to racism. His romantic friendship with his white schoolmate—Lloyd Bridges, who grins perpetually to establish an angelic temperament—floats on the latter's conviction that racism doesn't exist: "You either like a guy or you don't, that's all there is to it."

The film grows more contradictory: when the black man says that he's "different," he's repeatedly told by an army psychiatrist that everyone's "the same"—but it's also emphasized that he is hypersensitive. He's advised against "carrying that chip on your shoulder." However, "That sensitivity—that's the disease you've got—it's not your fault." The key racist in the movie is partially excused for psychological reasons: he "can't adjust" to the army, and "He's just thoughtless, he says things he doesn't mean." Above all, racists are "insecure." In short, racism might evaporate if blacks ceased to believe that they have suffered, and if whites would stop making jokes about fried chicken and watermelon and "high yaller women." Finally, a G.I. who's lost an arm in battle suggests that he's just as handicapped as the black soldier—as

James Edwards as the traumatized black soldier in Home of the Brave.

Intruder in the Dust: *Juano Hernandez in the custody of sheriff Will Geer.*

though society would subject a one-armed person to the same "discrimination" that it bestows on all black people.

Yet, despite its ambiguities, *Home of the Brave* has some absorbing passages, such as the dilating tensions before the soldiers embark on a dangerous mission. Their experience of hearing the screams of Lloyd Bridges when he's tortured offscreen is almost unbearably painful, as is the guilty anguish of the black at the death of his white friend. In spite of a pulsating score by Dmitri Tiomkin, complete with celestial choirs and operatic drum rolls, the movie does make one life lost represent the multiplicity of lives destroyed in an invasion: in that respect, the film is far more harrowing than a number of Forties war movies.

M-G-M was reluctant to produce Clarence Brown's movie of William Faulkner's *Intruder in the Dust* in 1949; by far the best of all of the racial films, it succeeds due to a superb script by Ben Maddow, the unassailable dignity of Juano Hernandez as the proud black man who's unjustly accused of murder, the rapt determination of the lynch mob, and because it approaches racism through the eyes of a young white boy discovering the hatred and suspicion that kindle his rural southern community. While the adults in movies like *Gentleman's Agreement* were startled to learn that racism is ugly, the boy's gradual education in that sphere endows the film with a maturity that its predecessors lacked. The black man seemed "too uppity" to Louis B. Mayer, and he was displeased because the character didn't remove his hat in the presence of white people. In fact, the producer's disapproval was a tribute to the movie, which demonstrated that many white citizens could not tolerate a black person who insisted on behaving like an equal, who refused to "act like a Negro."

Mayer said that the picture would be a failure, which it was, despite excellent reviews. Joseph Mankiewicz's *No Way Out* did almost as poorly in 1950; the low box-office returns on both movies led producers to conclude that the movie-goers who had responded enthusiastically to *Pinky* and *Home of the Brave* were "tired of" the issues, or else found them discomforting, by the time that the more outspoken movies were released. *No Way Out*, which gave Sidney Poitier his first screen role—as a black intern who is threatened with death after a white patient dies—had a fiercer candor than the earlier racial movies: when a throng of white men prepares to attack a black ghetto, the ensuing riot has a horrifying authenticity. But the film's angry vigor is occasionally diminished because the Poitier character is so much more intelligent and humane than those who want to destroy him that he seems to exist on an exalted moral plane. And the arch-racist is similar to the psychopath of *Crossfire:* others call him "a maniac," "a mad dog," and "a mental case" and vow that he's "not even human"—once again, racism belongs to the abnormal, not to ordinary American life.

Admittedly, it's easy to mock the naiveté of some of the racial movies of more than thirty years ago. But what perturbs us now had a flavoring of courage then—despite the paternalism that seeps through the spongy liberalism. Except for *Crossfire*, these films have uplift endings: the audience needn't leave the theater feeling upset. Moreover, the speeches that exalt "tolerance" couldn't have swayed anyone who didn't already agree with them, while the conclusions radiate a confidence about the future that's quite easy to reject. In the Forties, it didn't seem possible to cast *Pinky* with a black actress, or to acknowledge anti-Semitism as a national trait rather than as a tic of behavior, or to portray black "sensitivity" as rational rage. Historically, the compromises almost seem like fuel for perpetuating racism itself—even though the intentions of the film makers were certainly benign. However, very few would be able to follow them: the field that they had entered would soon become off limits.

•

After the 1947 hearings, films with moderately liberal trappings were censured, and *Variety* reported in 1948 that "studios are continuing to drop plans for 'message' pictures like hot coals." After all, the investigations had implied that patriotic producers should avoid social content. Even a conservative like John Ford was already uneasy because he had directed *The Grapes of Wrath*, which

No Way Out: *Richard Widmark, a deranged minor criminal, taunts Sidney Poitier while he examines the wounds of Widmark's brother (Dick Paxton).*

had been attacked by right-wingers in 1940. (Henry Fonda's final soliloquy, which promised that radicals would never cease to fight oppression, had vexed the anti-Communists, and Committee member Richard Nixon thought that the movie should not be sent to Yugoslavia.) Apart from the studios' frightened concern for what the public would "stand," it became reasonable to wonder what the Committee, or groups such as the American Legion, would condemn.

The Best Years of Our Lives (1946), the ultra-American weeper which nonetheless contained some robust social criticism, was rebuked by a friendly witness before the Committee because it depicted a bank's reluctance to give a veteran a G.I. loan. The witness referred to "the party line of making the returned soldier fear that the world is against him, that the American principle is against him, that business is against him. . . ." Five days later, director William Wyler remarked on the radio that he would no longer "be allowed" to make such a film, due to "the activities" of the Committee. He also doubted that Hollywood could continue to produce movies like *Crossfire* or *The Grapes of Wrath*.

Certainly, *The Best Years of Our Lives* didn't mesh with Ayn Rand's booklet, *Screen Guide for Americans*, which was published by the Motion Picture Alliance for the Preservation of American Ideals, and widely distributed throughout the studios. Rand's *Guide* warned: "Don't Smear Industrialists" and "Don't Smear the Free Enterprise System" and "Don't Smear Success." She also wrote: "Don't give your character—as a sign of villainy, as a damning characteristic—a desire to make money." And: "Don't ever use any lines about 'the common man' or 'the little people.' It is not the American idea to be either 'common' or 'little.' " Also: "Don't tell people that man is a helpless, twisted, drooling, snivelling, neurotic weakling. Show the world an *American* kind of man, for a change." Moreover: "It is the *moral* (no, not just political, but *moral*) duty of every decent man in the motion picture industry to throw into the ashcan, where it belongs, every story that smears industrialists as such."

The Best Years of Our Lives smeared no one. But it displayed the unsympathetic employers, insensitive relatives, and indifferent communities to which the veterans returned. Civilians keep urging the former fighting men to "forget" the war: "Snap out of it!" When banker Fredric March angrily upbraids his own company for its resistance to making loans to ex-G.I.s who have no collateral, it's plainly stated that the bank is threatening to deprive veterans of rights that were guaranteed by the government. Uneasy references to living with the atomic bomb, the priorities of finance that so swiftly replaced the war effort—"Last year, it was 'Kill Japs,' and this year, it's 'Make money,' " March declares with real revulsion—and the shortage of opportunities for those who need work, all add up to a definite critique of postwar society. A bitter air force hero is ready to throw away his citations after weeks of fruitless job-hunting, and a blusterer tells two veterans that we were "pushed" into the war "by a bunch of radicals in Washington," and that "we fought the wrong people, that's all."

Afflicted by giantism, the movie cannot spare us any kind of repetition: when two men get drunk, we have to see two protracted hangovers; in Robert E. Sherwood's script, the felicities or aggravations of any marriage are spelled out in monumental skywriting. (Still, March's fine performance as a traditional yet rebellious businessman, a semi-depressive who tries to be too hearty, sometimes rescues the film from its own turgidities.) The actresses in the movie have almost no function beyond tucking men into bed— this scene, evocative of a Freudian night nursery, occurs three times—and there are lunges into the ludicrous, as when Teresa Wright behaves as though one quick kiss in a parking lot were an extended orgy. That anyone could have viewed this film as even mildly radical was a signal that movie makers would have to prune their scenarios.

However, when the Committee announced that it was going to question Sherwood about *The Best Years of Our Lives*, producer

(OVERLEAF) *Veteran Fredric March inspects his prewar self in* The Best Years of Our Lives.

Samuel Goldwyn demanded that they furnish "facts," or else he would sue for damages. Some felt that Goldwyn's response helped to halt the 1947 investigations, although a larger share of the credit belonged to the Committee for the First Amendment, which had served to rally liberal and moderate newspapers and many public figures to protest the actions of the Committee. But the end of those hearings merely raised the curtain for the blacklist: the Hollywood Ten were fired a few weeks later.

•

The Senator Was Indiscreet (1947), written by Charles MacArthur, rewritten and produced by Nunnally Johnson, was the only film that George Kaufman ever directed. This very gentle satire—which Joseph McCarthy called "un-American" and "traitorous"—outlines the career of an incompetent senator (William Powell) who's unfit for any trade except running for president. The script reflects a Menckenish conviction that politicians are idiotic as well as corrupt. Powell takes a "firm" stand against assassination, promises two hundred dollars a week in Social Security to everyone, guarantees to send every citizen to Harvard, puts his relatives on his party's payroll, and piteously exclaims, "How could I know that that income tax bill meant me too?" The film spoofs the treacheries of the party regulars and luxuriates in the idea that a presidential candidate can be packaged and sold to the voters. (The movie also teases the Left: a sneering "Bolshevik waiter" derides "the capitalistic press" and scolds the senator for including "not one word in defense of Yugoslavia" in his speeches.) As a child, I watched some of the scenes being shot and can testify that the joviality on the set was not a front for political conspiracy. The film makers' most urgent conferences focused on Ella Raines's tendency to fluff her lines during speeches that required rapid delivery.

Nunnally Johnson was astounded by the uproar that arose even before *The Senator Was Indiscreet* was released. At a screening, Clare Boothe Luce—whom he'd known for years—asked loudly, "Was this picture made by an American?" *Life*, which had reviewed the movie favorably, then retracted that view in a column called "On Second Thought," which revealed the film's latent un-Americanism. The apolitical Johnson, one of Hollywood's wittiest screenwriters, had never imagined that his new comedy would be incendiary; however, not long before its opening, one of the founders of the Motion Picture Alliance for the Preservation of American Ideals had told the Committee, "where you see a little drop of cyanide in a picture, a small grain of arsenic, something that makes every Senator, every businessman, every employer a crook . . . that is Communistic!" The film was attacked by the American Legion and in many editorials. The Eastern Pennsylvania and Rocky Mountain Units of the Allied Theater Owners stated that "the picture will be recommended highly by *Pravda* and the party line. . . . We should remember the adverse propaganda of the prewar and early war period that Germany and Italy used against us by presenting *Mr. Smith Goes to Washington, The Grapes of Wrath, Tobacco Road,* and gangster and crime films as true portrayals of American life."

In the Forties, the government showed an increasing concern for our reputation as it was conveyed through movies, and a 1945 memorandum from the State Department had warned against exports "which create erroneous impressions about the United States." In light of that consideration, the Motion Picture Association of America—which had initially given its approval to the script of *The Senator Was Indiscreet*—forbade its being shown overseas. (The Association was a trade organization that imposed self-censorship—in order to prevent outside interference or boycotts from groups like the Catholic Legion of Decency.) Prior to the war, the studios had had a limited relationship with the government; the producers contributed money to political campaigns and expected reciprocal favors—as when they needed to film battleships or army installations. Mutual cooperation was naturally intensified in wartime, since the film executives wanted military deferments or commissions for their stars, as well as footage for extensive combat scenes. The habit of concurrence continued after the war, when the industry was highly dependent on profits from foreign markets, and the government strenuously promoted American movies abroad. Hence protecting the national image was almost as important to Hollywood as it was to the State Department, which deduced that films that made Americans appear frivolous or hyper-criminal were detrimental to diplomacy—as was any movie that suggested that our political leaders might be imperfect.

II: *The Perils of Patriotism*

With a lurch of hindsight, several films of 1943 were examined for political taint in 1947. Movies that had been considered patriotic during the war were branded as subversive four years later. *Mission to Moscow*, directed by Michael Curtiz, was based on Joseph Davies's best seller, which had been serialized in the *Reader's Digest*—a rather rum context for a narrative that was so flattering to the Soviet Union, where Davies was ambassador from 1936 to 1938. J. Parnell Thomas was certain that the government had pressured Warner Brothers to produce the movie, and that it was federally subsidized, but Jack Warner denied that when Thomas questioned him.

However, Warner wrote in his 1965 memoirs that Roosevelt did ask him to make the film—in theory, to help to persuade Stalin not to make a second pact with Hitler if Russia suffered losses on "major fronts" due to a shortage of ammunition. Warner claimed that he was "powerfully disturbed," but "I considered FDR's request an order." (*Mission to Moscow* was written by Howard Koch; the Warners told him that the president felt that the movie was very important to the war effort. Later an uncooperative witness, Koch had never been a Communist, but he was blacklisted anyway—mainly because of Jack Warner's testimony, in which the

57

producer tried to blame the screenwriter for the pro-Soviet aspects of the film.) Davies later took prints of the picture to Moscow, and Stalin endorsed the movie for distribution throughout the Soviet Union. Still, apart from Warner's self-serving autobiography, there is no solid evidence that Roosevelt himself "requested" the production, and skepticism seems reasonable. But many in Hollywood did believe that the government had inspired the gargantuan mashnote to our ally, and the Warners' studio tended to make films that upheld Roosevelt's policies. It was rumored that Ivy Litvinov, whose husband was then the Soviet ambassador to the United States, had been an unofficial adviser for the movie. The technical adviser was Jay Leyda, the film historian and critic who had worked as an assistant to Eisenstein.

Davies, an ambitious naïf who knew very little about Russia until he arrived there, remained an enthusiastic capitalist who did not think that the Communist system could endure. However, Davies's belief that an alliance with the Soviets was crucial to the defeat of Hitler, and his commitment to negotiating with Stalin, was as acceptable during the war as it was repellent to prewar isolationists and postwar anti-Communists. Davies also credited the Soviets with a better and earlier understanding of the Nazis than the Allies. Much of the movie builds toward an explanation of the Nazi-Soviet Pact of 1939. Britain, characterized by the reactionaries of the Chamberlain government, and France are blamed for failing to enter on a policy of collective security. Stressing that the Russians feel that the Allies are rejecting them, the ambassador warns: "If the democracies continue to look down their noses at Russia . . . they'll drive Stalin into Hitler's arms!" (Along with the Left, some moderates did take that view of the Pact, which the movie interprets in terms of self-defense once "Stalin was left standing alone against Hitler.") After the German invasion of Russia, when Roosevelt, Churchill, and George Marshall expected the Russians to lose swiftly, Davies firmly predicted that the Red Army would perform very well—contradicting the military experts who said that Moscow would fall in six weeks.

Otherwise, this docu-drama does merit J. Edgar Hoover's

charge that it was "a prostitution of historical fact." The Moscow trials of 1937 and 1938 are garbled together into one event, so that Radek and Bukharin appear in the same courtroom—when they were actually tried a year apart—along with Marshal Tukhachevsky, who had been shot without a public hearing nine months before the Bukharin-Krestinsky-Yagoda trial. Hearing a dead man testify does add spice to the movie, especially since his lines are really the words of the accused Muralov.

The film insists on the guilt of the defendants in conspiring to kill the officials of the Kremlin and to overthrow the Soviet government with the aid of Germany and Japan, a plot which would "lead to eventual war with the United States," according to the movie, not Davies himself. The film makes Vyshinsky a humane prosecutor, patiently listening to the mournful or brazen confessions of sabotage and espionage with the goal of "assisting foreign aggressors in defeating and dismembering" the Soviet Union. (George Kennan, who was Davies's interpreter, recalled "hissing into his ear . . . a simultaneous translation of Vyshinsky's thundering brutalities" and "the delicate innuendos" of the accused.) Davies's memoirs prove that he was "reluctantly" convinced that the Soviet government had proved its case. But he was also appalled by the purges of the Stalin regime—whereas his movie-self accepts them calmly. As soon as the defendants are sentenced to death, the film shifts hastily to some pleasing parachute displays, thus skirting the messy topic of executions.

The release of *Mission to Moscow* brought attacks from Westbrook Pegler, anti-Soviet pickets outside the theaters, and some outraged letters to *The New York Times* from philosopher John Dewey and Suzanne La Folette, secretary to Dewey's International Committee of Inquiry into the Moscow Trials of 1937–1938, and a scorching correspondence followed. Dewey was disgusted by the movie's falsification of the trials, and because the film gave "the impression that Stalin is killing off not only potential political opponents but traitors in the service of foreign powers." One writer retorted that Walter Duranty, the *Times*'s Pulitzer prize-winning Moscow correspondent, had believed that "substantial justice was

Krestinsky (Roman Bohnen) confesses his guilt at the Moscow trials in Mission to Moscow.

rendered in the trials." The passions of the period erupted in the ensuing exchange, amid vehement demands for "objectivity" on both sides.

•

From the moment when FDR—a faceless figure, reduced to an arm pouring tea and a disembodied voice—orders Davies (Walter Huston) to Moscow, much of the movie is relentless comedy. In no other film have I seen so many spinning globes—the props most essential to *Mission to Moscow*; again and again, world leaders pensively twirl the spheres on their desks while asserting that peace (or war) is possible. There are also glimpses of stationary globes. The Germans are represented by a few officials given to chortling, "The Americans have become very naive—heh, heh, heh!" or announcing, "The trains of the new Germany wait for no one!" All the Russian leaders have beautiful manners—they usually wear white tie and tails—and the ambassador isn't ruffled by the notion that his embassy may be bugged (an idea that horrified the real Davies).

Beaming at parades of tanks and troops, the ambassador's family basks in the affabilities of Soviet social life. We hear snippets of chat between the hors d'oeuvres at embassy balls: "How are things in Geneva?" and "You Russians are always hearing the drums of war" and "There's time to walk the tightrope between great powers," as the Japanese and Chinese diplomats snub each other and the other nations waltz harmoniously. More globes are spun. The American ambassador tells Stalin, "I believe, Sir, that history will record you as a great benefactor of mankind"—which was not in Davies's book, although he did write that Stalin's "brown eye is exceedingly gentle and kind. A child would like to sit in his lap and a dog would sidle up to him."

George Kennan has written that Davies pretended—for the sake of "personal publicity" at home—that the Soviet-American relationship was far more affectionate than it actually was, and his staff felt that he misled the State Department about the activities of the Kremlin. (Some thought that Davies hoped to be an eventual candidate for the presidency.) Still, although the editors of Davies's book cut his most disparaging remarks about the Soviet Union, he did denounce the police state, as the movie never does. As the Allies finally prepare for "the People's war," the film ends with a vision of a transparent city rising against the clouds, while a voice makes pledges to "unborn generations" and then asks, "Am I my brother's keeper?" A throaty chorus sings in reply, "Yes! You are! You are, yes, you are, your brother's keeper. Now and forever more."

Revolution isn't mentioned in the movie, nor is Communism. The director's principal achievement was forcing Walter Huston to speak quickly; however, Huston appeared to be trailing many habits from *Abraham Lincoln* and *Dodsworth*. James Agee's reflections on *Mission to Moscow* are still apt: ". . . the film is almost describable as the first Soviet production to come from a major American studio. Almost, but not quite. For it is indeed, as Manny Farber has well said, a mishmash: of Stalinism with New Dealism with Hollywoodism with journalism with shaky experimentalism. . . ."

Agee emphasized that the movie marked "the first time that moving pictures have even flexed their muscles in a human crisis." But since the film misrepresents much of Davies's book, it's astonishing to see him appearing in the prologue, praising "those fine and patriotic citizens, the Warner brothers." Still, his ear wasn't finely tuned to nuance, let alone distortion; Edmund Wilson called him "the greatest master of bad official English since the late President Harding." And it's true that Davies's style rarely disappoints: in April 1938, he wrote, "Things sure have been popping here since our arrival. . . . There is never a dull moment in Moscow."

•

The natural exuberance of the Russian people in *Mission to Moscow* is exceeded only by their ungirdled gaiety in *Song of Russia*, which was directed by Gregory Ratoff in 1944, written by Richard Collins—who later gave twenty-three names to the Committee—

Mission to Moscow: *Stalin (Manart Kippen) explains a point to Churchill (Dudley Field Malone).*

and Paul Jarrico, who was blacklisted after Collins and others had named him. In order to make a movie that would pay tribute to the Russian resistance, just as *Mrs. Miniver* had exalted the heroism of our British allies, M-G-M had bought a property called *Scorched Earth*. Those who worked on the film were told that the government had urged the studio to produce it—which they believed, because it was so unlikely that Louis B. Mayer (an arch-conservative and keen Republican) would have initiated a pro-Soviet movie. The two Communist screenwriters expected to make a deeply serious film about the Russians destroying their crops and villages in order to deny any sustenance to the invading German troops. Anna Louise Strong, the journalist devoted to the Soviet cause, was hired as an adviser—although she contributed almost nothing to the final script. But the movie was produced by Joe Pasternak, whose specialty was Deanna Durbin musicals, such as *Three Smart Girls* and *Mad About Music*. Conflict between these mutually bewildered factions continued during the shooting of the film. The final product suggests that scorching the earth was a tuneful procedure, also that Russia would be saved by the harmonies of Tchaikovsky.

Ayn Rand, in her testimony before the Committee, was not inaccurate when she protested that there was too much smiling throughout the movie. As a Russian emigré who had left her country in 1926, after her family had lost the property it had acquired in Czarist Russia, Rand also objected to the scores of radios owned by M-G-M's peasants, and to their access to long-distance telephones. Actually, the Russians in this film are quite like the movie-Negroes in an earlier Hollywood: a jubilant race, addicted to music and laughter, blessed with inborn rhythm. From the singing farmers who stride from the fields with hoes aloft on their shoulders to the frolicking children and the high-kicking peasant women in spike heels who cut loose with the Charleston in a church—"a traditional Russian wedding dance"—the Soviet citizens seem to be bathed in a disproportionate bliss.

Robert Taylor first told the Committee that he had reluctantly appeared in the movie because the Office of War Information had wanted M-G-M to make it, and that he was kept from joining the navy until the project was finished. He later retracted the statement that he had been "forced" into the role. But his remorse for having starred in the picture was highlighted by his eagerness to identify several persons who were "reputedly fellow travelers or possibly Communists."

In *Song of Russia*, Taylor was cast as a distinguished American conductor touring the Soviet Union before the Nazi invasion—in fact, during the period of the Pact, although the film admits to no alliance between Stalin and Hitler. He conducts our national anthem as though he were serving a series of tennis balls, and the scene dissolves from New York to Moscow, where a Soviet band continues "The Star-Spangled Banner" beneath a hammer and sickle. ("That," said Ayn Rand, "made me sick.") Laslo Benedek, the assistant producer, was later accused of conspiring to impel American audiences to rise for their anthem and to therefore remain standing in the presence of the red flag—while the soundtrack switched to the Russian anthem. M-G-M had hoped that Greta Garbo would play the female lead, particularly because her involvement with conductor Leopold Stokowski would enhance the publicity for the picture, but Garbo didn't comply.

Taylor's romance with peasant Susan Peters results in dinner in an opulent nightclub where he exclaims, "I can't get over it! Everyone seems to be having such a good time!"—instead of "brooding about their souls," as Russians are reputed to do. Their rapture peaks with his discovery that she is "just like an American girl": indeed, the whole movie alleges that Russia and America are spiritual twins. When the Russians knock on wood, it's explained as "an old Slavic custom." Taylor is smitten with the entire country, especially after Tchaikovsky "did something to me way deep down inside."

Visiting the heroine at her parents' farm, where she repairs ploughs and drives a tractor in a ruffled blouse and fresh lipstick,

(OVERLEAF) *Joyful peasants in* Song of Russia.

he's soon voluptuously sifting grain through his fingers with her father, who appears to be a Yiddish comic from Manhattan's Lower East Side. Due to M-G-M's vigilance, the screenwriters were not allowed to indicate that these happy peasants worked on a collective farm, and they had to cut the word "community" from their script. As in *The North Star* (1943), the Russian farmers revel in the delusion that they own their land: there are many fond references to "our soil" and "our earth."

The lovers are married in a local church by a benevolent priest. When the Germans invade, tour manager Robert Benchley babbles, "Down at the Consulate, they're saying the Nazis will win the war in six weeks!" Complying with Stalin's request that everyone give their "full dewotion to the defense of our fatherland," Peters rushes off to her "anti-parachute work"—making Molotov cocktails from vodka bottles—and Benchley recalls how his forebears in Lexington, Massachusetts, "also fought to defend their country"—another line that infuriated Ayn Rand. (One member of the Committee reminded her that we might have lost the war without Russia's help, but she brushed that thought aside.) The movie suggests that the Nazis are dreadful because they have separated the newlyweds. And yet the film is momentarily touching—when the Russians burn their own towns. Finally, Taylor and Peters are sent home to preach the message of the Soviets to America: "We are soldiers side by side—in this fight for all humanity." In sum, *Song of Russia* is a delectably bad movie, and *The New York Times* may be forgiven for calling it "a honey of a topical musical film."

·

Ayn Rand was especially incensed by the spurts of Christianity throughout the movie, and she told the Committee that a Communist who had "anything to do with religion" would be expelled from the Party. However, some of the Communist screenwriters weren't at all shy of God. In *Action in the North Atlantic* (1943), written by John Howard Lawson with additional dialogue by Alvah Bessie—two of the Hollywood Ten—the deity is almost overworked: a character affirms, "I got faith: in God, in President Roosevelt, and the Brooklyn Dodgers, in that order of their importance," and when Raymond Massey, shouting defiantly at a submarine crammed with Germans, is told that they can't hear him, he replies, "No, but God can."

The movie, a hymn to the merchant marine, has only one line that tilts even faintly toward the Left: a seaman refers to a Russian plane as "one of ours." Otherwise, like *Cloak and Dagger*, an ode to the CIA's predecessor, the OSS—written by Albert Maltz and Ring Lardner, Jr., who were also among the Ten— *Action in the North Atlantic* proves that almost no one wrote more passionately patriotic movies than American Communists did in wartime. (The Party, which was dissolved on May 22, 1944, became the Communist Political Association until July 29, 1945, and the CPA's slogan was "Communism is Twentieth Century Americanism.") Most of the combat films were scripted during the period when the organization was thoroughly committed to the war effort, when Earl Browder, the national chairman, called for total support of Roosevelt's policies at home and abroad. *The Report on Blacklisting*, commissioned by the Fund for the Republic and written by John Cogley, which later confirmed that there were no traces of Communism in the 159 movies that the Ten worked on before they were blacklisted, did note that a few were "over zealous" in their treatment of "war content."

Tender Comrade—Robert Louis Stevenson's term for a wife— directed by Edward Dmytryk and written by Dalton Trumbo in 1944, is probably the most asphyxiating of the wartime uplift movies. Ginger Rogers rents a house with several women who work at

(OVERLEAF) *Bombardier Dana Andrews will fight the Nazis with the assistance of young Russian guerrillas Jane Withers, Anne Baxter, and Farley Granger in Lewis Milestone's* The North Star *(1943). Retitled* Armored Attack, *the pro-Soviet movie was later prefaced with the explanation that the Russians were once our allies, but had ceased to be.*

an aircraft factory while their husbands fight overseas; they divide expenses and take votes on all decisions. Regarding their domestic arrangements, Kim Hunter says, "Share and share alike—isn't that right?" Mady Christians nods and answers: "Democracy." This exchange displeased Rogers's mother, who scrutinized scripts at RKO and was supposed to be attuned to "hidden" Communist propaganda, as though it were a whistle that only a dog could hear. (She also objected to Clifford Odets's *None But the Lonely Heart*, citing *The Hollywood Reporter*'s remark that the musical score by Hanns Eisler was "moody and somber throughout in the Russian manner." And when Odets scripted *Deadline at Dawn*, she detected Communist inspiration in a comic line that implied that it was a crime not to be a success.)

Perhaps Trumbo and Dmytryk—both members of the Ten— thought that they were abetting feminism by depicting women coping with life on their own. However, the heroines of *Tender Comrade* are hopeless at economics, lumpish in debate—"Gee, aren't men fools?" "Yes, but aren't they sweet?"—and feebly dependent on talking to photographs of their husbands. Strumming on their pride in the men who serve their country, most resist "lunchstand Romeos," but the movie would have been much more interesting if the Motion Picture Code had allowed the women to discuss sexual deprivation, which does pervade the atmosphere of the film.

Flashbacks transport us to Ginger Rogers's life with Robert Ryan—here wrenched away from his normal role as a grinning psychopath to participate in one of the most bizarre marriages ever idealized on the screen. He assails her for using his razor, she berates him for rings in the bathtub. But their savage brawls are projected as beguiling spats. When Rogers weeps, there seems to be a recurring problem of the sinus cavities; for a dancer, she flounces badly. They decide to postpone parenthood because "It wouldn't be fair on the little guy to be born in wartime." Nonetheless, Rogers becomes pregnant during a night when she sleeps on a chair while he "hogs" the bed; it's tempting to deduce that sex occurred standing up or on the floor.

Susan Peters teaches Robert Taylor to fire a machine gun in Song of Russia.

However, her garrulous lecture to her baby, after she receives word of her husband's death—"He went out and died so that you could have a better break than he did. . . . He died for a good thing, little guy, and if you ever betray it, you might as well be dead too. . . . Don't ever let anybody say he died for nothing, Chris boy"—suggests that she cherishes the man in death as much as she loathed him in life. Unstrung by patriotic grief, she also seems to have switched babies: the infant in this scene bears small resemblance to the one seen earlier. Still, she promises the little stranger that it will "have a wonderful century," thanks to its father's demise. As the work of a Communist screenwriter, *Tender Comrade* seems to suggest that Americans are invincible—and that their only enemies are the ones they marry.

•

Audiences of 1949 may have been startled to hear that "the world is perishing from an orgy of self-sacrificing." But only those who had read the 754 pages of Ayn Rand's *The Fountainhead* could have followed the tormented logic of her script, which is riddled with the themes of her "objectivist" philosophy. The screen version, directed by King Vidor, can be revered as one of the funniest films of any period. Gary Cooper is the architectural genius whom the public hates because he's a "visionary" and a devout "individualist." Wicked "collectivists," who announce that "there's no place for originality" and who pander to "the rule of the mob," demand that he compromise in designing his buildings: we see the hands of his enemies adding Doric porticoes, pediments, and colonial trimmings to the models of his skyscrapers. Since his work resembles the Los Angeles airport combined with the visions of the early Uris brothers, the result is breath-stopping. Refusing to "conform," he protects the integrity of his art by dynamiting a housing project that deviates from his original plans. Finally, he triumphs over the "parasites" who conspire to "enslave" his gifts and to "break the spirits" of his kindred geniuses, aiming to reduce them to "robots . . . without will, hope, or dignity." Presumably, his unique talents flourished to produce masterpieces like the Americana Hotel and the General Motors Building.

Gary Cooper as the master builder in The Fountainhead. *King Vidor had hoped to engage Frank Lloyd Wright as a consultant for the film, but Jack Warner vetoed the idea.*

Although it was built on a best seller, the film was a financial failure—even though Rand, who organized salons in Hollywood and elsewhere to educate her disciples about the horrors of liberalism, already had a substantial following. It seems improbable that many movie-goers of the Forties would have recognized *The Fountainhead* as a right-wing movie, since the ardent anti-Communism of the novel was so clumsily adapted for the screen. But some members of the Hollywood Left found it far from comic: to them, it seemed like a symbol of what lay ahead—a further tightening of the forces of reaction. In the book, any whiff of "altruism" or "self-sacrifice" is equivalent to totalitarianism, and "equality" is really "slavery." (One catches the drift when a villain says, "The noblest conception on earth is man's absolute equality.") In fact, "selfless" means Communist—and those who call themselves "intellectuals" are notoriously unselfish.

The movie contains only some of the ferocious disgust that animates the novel: disgust for "the masses," for the inferior, and for those who "organize" them. The hero and the heroine are presented as chips off a master race, and they're biologically superior to others—whereas evil always has a lamentable physique. It's intimated that the weak deserve to be destroyed, and it's clear that they deserve to suffer.

Rand, who venerates ruthlessness, is contradictory about power, which she praises when it's allied to making money, but deplores when it means "ruling" others—as though old-fashioned laissez-faire capitalism (which she extols) never partook of a pecking order. Her master folk assert that they don't want to dominate anyone, yet they are blazing authoritarians who impose their wills on everyone else. Meanwhile, sexual suffering and brutality are glorified: "She had found joy in her revulsion, in her terror and his strength. That was the degradation she had wanted. . . ." These are piquant themes to enlist in the cause of human rights, especially since contempt is the strongest emotion of the leading characters: they despise most of their fellow citizens, whom Rand makes despicable as well as inferior. Rage courses through her work: no one can be weak or mediocre or mistaken without being depraved as well. Denouncing oppression, she recommends an oppressive society. In her one-woman war against tyranny, she writes at times like a quasi-anarchist. But in other passages, she enshrines dictatorial temperaments.

Even though all of these ideas don't reach the screen intact, Rand's paramilitary romanticism—often seasoned with self-punishment—billows through the film. Patricia Neal and Cooper collaborate on a sadomasochistic passion in which rape is more satisfying than "surrender." Neal first glimpses Cooper laboring in a granite quarry: she immediately falls in love with his drill, which flashes back in her fantasies when she's gazing into her mirror. Before they're socially introduced, she slashes his face with a riding crop—a sign of overwhelming attraction. In the novel, these two often "lean against" the sky or the air, which may account for the odd postures assumed by the performers in this movie, where Neal has difficulty in staying on her feet.

Once Neal examines Cooper's work, she dotes on his spire as much as on his drill. He becomes more passive as she grows more amorous—"I loved you," he says drearily, "the first moment I ever saw you"—and he doesn't even seem to enjoy watching her flog her horse. Dithering and blinking, he can only raise an eyebrow as she bares her teeth. When she evokes her "burning desire" for him, he listens politely while gazing into space, and then responds with all the sexuality of an ironing board. Otherwise, he tugs at his lapels to convey individuality. The movie climaxes as the book does—with the heroine soaring upward in an outdoor elevator on her beloved's tallest creation: he stands on top of the erection of his palace of fallacies, while she gazes worshipfully at his body outlined against the sky.

The collectivist scoundrels of *The Fountainhead* promote bad art—"a vicious fraud"—in order to destroy all standards and then to "control the world." Sublime works of art, however, cannot fall short of perfection. One wonders how Rand applied her code of aesthetics to her own prose. Her vast fictional samplers were embroidered in the style of the pulp magazines of the late Forties: "Nothing but your body, that mouth of yours, and the way your eyes would look at me if. . . ." No doubt she felt that her detractors were simply opposed to her ideology, and that those who valued beauty as much as truth would admire such sentences as: "She knew that a continuous struggle against the compulsion of a single desire was a compulsion also, but it was the form she preferred to accept," or "I want you—I want you like an animal, or a cat on a fence, or a whore." But much of Rand's audience must have been as confounded by her artistic credo as Gary Cooper looked when he had to struggle with such lines as "A building has integrity, just like a man—and just as seldom," or "There is no such thing as a collective brain."

Rand's political convictions undoubtedly eluded many who throbbed to the novel or went to the movie. But the studios were already beginning to produce some films whose content she must have esteemed: *The Red Menace, Red Nightmare, The Red Danube, Red Snow, Invasion U.S.A., I Married a Communist,* and *Red Planet Mars.*

And what about *I Married a Monster from Outer Space* which managed to combine anti-communist fears with gay-bashing. The husband (and his alien buddies) won't have anything to do with women or alcohol and hang out with one another. A hilarious flick.

III: *Penance*
and Assault

In 1947, Richard Nixon asked Eric Johnston, the president of the Motion Picture Producers Association, and Jack Warner, if any anti-Communist films were being made, and J. Parnell Thomas prodded Louis B. Mayer with the same query. None were in production at that time, although Mayer cited *Ninotchka* (1939) and *Comrade X* (1940), which had ridiculed the Soviet Union before it was an ally. (At the request of the State Department, *Ninotchka* had been sent to Italy after the war; it was credited with helping to influence an election there which some feared the Communists might win. And it was hastily re-released here in 1947, one month after the hearings.) Other friendly witnesses before the Committee—such as Robert Taylor and Gary Cooper—were repeatedly asked if the studios should make anti-Communist pictures similar to the earlier anti-Nazi movies, and they agreed heartily that the industry ought to comply.

Adolphe Menjou said that such films "would be an incredible success." In fact, most were financial disasters, leading *Variety* to conclude in the fall of 1949 that "the public will buy message pix, but they gotta be good." However, the movies were re-run as second features on double bills; hence they were widely seen even

CF. HANS CONREID'S DAFT CAMEO IN BIG JIM McCLAIN.

though they had not initially been profitable. And, for certain film makers, being asked to work on an anti-Communist picture was like a loyalty test: if someone who was thought to be a Communist refused to participate in the project, it was assumed that he must be a Party member. So, for some writers, directors, and actors, taking part in a film such as *I Married a Communist* was rather like receiving clearance—it meant that they were politically clean.

According to the Cogley *Report on Blacklisting*, the number of movies concerning other social issues decreased drastically between 1947 and 1954, although more than fifty anti-Communist films were produced. Most were shot on low budgets with non-stars—indicating that the studios did not expect them to earn well. Apparently, the producers hoped to satisfy their right-wing critics without losing money; films that evoked any kind of ideology were usually unpopular, and the executives dreaded deficits when the movie business was already wounded by competition from television. Hence cheap films were hastily made in order to rinse the industry's image of radicalism during the Cold War: they were part of Hollywood's ritual of atonement and appeasement, and were aimed at an uninformed audience in a decade when almost anything that middle America feared could be related to Communism. Perhaps in no other period have such dismal creations been launched as a form of public relations.

All the beaming and twinkling and the handsome profiles of *Song of Russia* and *The North Star* were negated by *The Iron Curtain* (1948), *The Red Menace* (1949), *I Was a Communist for the FBI* (1951), *The Whip Hand* (1951), *Walk East on Beacon* (1952), and *My Son John* (1952). These movies instruct us especially on how American Communists look: most are apt to be exceptionally haggard or disgracefully pudgy. Occasionally, they're effeminate: a man who wears gloves shouldn't be trusted. However, in films that feature dauntless FBI agents, it's very difficult to tell them apart from the enemy, since both often lurk on street corners in raincoats and identical snap-brims while pretending to read newspapers, and also because many B-actors lack distinguishing features: they simply look alike. Just when you assume that the miscreants are massing to plot, they turn out to be the heroes. But you can sometimes spot a Communist because his shadow looms larger and blacker than his adversary's. Also, movie-Communists walk on a forward slant, revealing their dedication to the cause. Now and then, they're elegantly dressed, equipped with canes and stick-pins—which prove them hypocrites. But most are scruffy.

In many of these movies, there's a figure whom my notes identify as the Bad Blonde: in the Fifties, you knew that there was something terribly wrong with a woman if her slip straps showed through her blouse; in this context, it meant treason. Bad blondes tend to order triple bourbons or to be hooked on absinthe, and they often seduce "impressionable" young men into joining the Party. Communists also debase chaste American institutions—by meeting in the Boston Public Gardens amid the swanboats, or by carrying a copy of the *Reader's Digest* or a TWA flight bag in order to recognize each other—and they do frightful things to flags. Bereft of humor, they grimly demand explanations of "jokes," and are incapable of asking civil questions, except when they're offering "More Scotch?" to a possible recruit; otherwise, they always bark when they want to know something. Moreover, Communists are cruel to animals. (But we don't know how they treat children, since they never have any. Perhaps that was meant to reassure the public: Communists don't literally breed.) Often, they can be detected by their style of exhaling: they expel smoke very slowly from their nostrils before threatening someone's life, or suggesting that "harm" will come to his family. Recurrently, Hollywood employed the formula of substituting Communists for gangsters—hence the public could feel at home with the familiar image of the criminal.

Communists "never keep their promises," and they're likely to go berserk when they're arrested. But they devote so much time to spying on each other that it's hard to see how they could have any free time for serious espionage. While almost all are raving villains, a few are permitted "reasons" for joining the Party, such as the Depression or fighting fascism abroad, and a couple were snared by their own "idealism." These movies dispense the fantasy

Thomas Gomez as the murderous Communist Party leader—who was meant to suggest Harry Bridges—in Robert Stevenson's I Married a Communist *(1950). The script asserts that "one Party member can indoctrinate a thousand."*

that when such souls repent and try to resign, their comrades either expose their membership to the FBI—so that they'll be jailed or deported—or kill them.

Above all, the fictional Communists are murderers, particularly of their own kind: they don't hesitate to hurl their associates in front of trains or out of windows, or to "hound" them to suicide. History is unfurled as proof: "You know what happens to traitors: Trotsky thought he was safe—but they got to him." In *I Married a Communist* (1950)—a savage smear on Harry Bridges, which shows the West Coast Longshoremen's and Warehousemen's Union being ruled by Communists—the Party underlings toss an informer off a dock and then smile faintly while he drowns slowly. (But some Communists dispatch others with scant provocation: if an innocent merely says that he doesn't like them.) During *Big Jim McLain* (1952)—where John Wayne pursues Communists in Honolulu—"unstable" Party members are given inoculations that render them too witless to testify before the Committee; the weaklings had already succumbed to whiskey or nervous breakdowns due to the "torment" of following the Party line. The Communist leaders also plan to slay their "expendable" followers whose idealism makes them "useless" to the Party. All in all, the movies suggest that Communists were so adept at eliminating one another that there was little work or glory left for the FBI.

These films wrench one back to the issues that swirled around *Mission to Moscow*. James Agee referred to that picture as "nominal nonfiction whose responsibilities, whose power for good or evil, enlightenment or deceit, are appalling." He reflected that "It is good to see the Soviet Union shown as the one nation during the past decade which not only understood fascism but desired to destroy it, and which not only desired peace but had some ideas how it might be preserved. . . ." As for the rest, he called it "shameful rot," because it indulged in "the all but universal custom of using only so much of the truth as may be convenient" and disdained "verisimilitude." But, although *Mission to Moscow* made hash out of facts, it didn't soar to the extremes that the anti-

+ beats hell out of

BJM is notable for its (literal) equation of communism with leprosy and little people. Once again, this film has the bright commie son turning against his humble parents who turn him in [to] the BJM + co.

Also cf. Wayne's dismissal of "psychological" explanations for left-leaning.

When I showed BJM at Amherst College in 1977, students were more bemused than amused and found my guffaws and gasps a bit much.

Communist films did. The pro-Soviet movie, for all its transgressions, sought to promote cordiality abroad—at a time when many welcomed Russia on our side—while the red-flogging movies tried to inspire hatred at home. When one ponders the responsibility of film makers, there's a forcible difference between whitewashing a wartime ally and portraying American "subversives" as killers.

•

"We'll have our way, even if it means blood! shed! and terror!": perhaps the choicest of the anti-Communist films, *The Red Menace*, was directed by R. G. Springsteen, who had made twenty-five Roy Rogers movies, and released "with unusual pride" by Republic, a studio that specialized in monster pictures. The film's shoddiness reveals its cynicism. Here, California Communists use sex for enticement: a potential dupe says to the bad blonde, "I always thought the Commies peddled bunk. I didn't know they came as cute as you." She lets him kiss her, then pulls away to hand him *Das Kapital.* Later, when they hit the sheets, we assume that he has read some key passages. But he rapidly discovers that many of his new comrades are pining to leave the Party. When a black member—who's exploited in his job at "The Toiler," their official newspaper—does depart, a leader snarls, "We're wasting our time on these *African ingrates!*" (These Communists are multi-racists: an Italian who asks an irreverent question is rebuked as "a Mussolini-spawned Dago.") A poet is expelled for writing "politically objectionable" verses—"We contend that Marx had no basis in Hegel!"—and he's "driven" to kill himself.

The movie illustrates that Communists crack easily: there's a marvelous mad scene where a prime Party theorist is besieged by imaginary drumbeats while being politely questioned by the Department of Justice. She yells, "You're too late . . . ! Our ammunition is already here." The soundtrack rumbles: we too begin to hear the drums. "The legions—they're entering the city! In a few minutes they'll be here. And they'll stand you up against the wall—" The drums crash even more loudly. "Hear them!" She laughs deliriously. "You fools! Don't you hear them!" As she's led out frothing, one bemused pin-striped suit says to another, "We only wanted her statement for clarification."

Apart from contagious insanity, the Communists' fiercest problem is rampant inefficiency. Even "the Party doom squad" fails to capture a disaffected couple. Since most of the faithful are overweight, their fist fights with their victims—also flabby—are painful to witness. Throughout, the actors have trouble with words like "invidious" and "insidious." These films prove that Americans can always outsmart the "Red vermin"—whether the heroes are the modest citizens of a small town or members of a federal agency. In *The Whip Hand,* a wholesome vacationing journalist— who has to utter such lines as "What goes on around here?"— unmasks a vile Communist scheme to demolish this country by germ warfare. "Within the next forty-eight hours, America will sink to its knees!" We've often heard that our nation has a heart, but it's hard to visualize its elbows or its knees.

The Red Menace was narrated by Lloyd G. Douglas, a bona fide member of the Los Angeles City Council, and the voice-over is charged with feeling as he points out that a character "has fallen prey to Marxian hatred and strategy intent on spreading world dissension and treason, unaware that he is only the tool of men who would destroy his country." Douglas keeps explaining the film to us—in case we don't quite grasp what's happening on the screen. This quasi-documentary style, employed in other anti-Communist movies, loaned authority to their lavish distortions. *The Iron Curtain,* which claimed to be adapted from "a true story, authenticated by the Royal Canadian Mounted Police," cast Dana Andrews as a Soviet code clerk; his performance confirms that being Russian means having a congenital case of the sulks. While the movie was being shot, visitors were barred from the set, and those who worked on it were almost quarantined. *The Iron Curtain* was written by Milton Krims, who co-scripted *Confessions of a Nazi Spy* (1939), which became a model for the Cold War films. The movie remains utterly suspenseless as the protagonists scamper about trying to save their own lives, but Bosley Crowther of *The New York Times* called it "highly inflammatory" and "dangerous." He concluded that this "conventional hiss-the-villain" picture "would pass for a mild spy melodrama if it weren't for the violence of its blast."

Crowther also found *I Was a Communist for the FBI* (directed by Gordon Douglas) "horrendous" for its "reckless 'red' smears." The film was "based on the story of" Matthew Cvetic, which was ghostwritten for *The Saturday Evening Post*. The real Cvetic was for seven years an undercover agent recruited by J. Edgar Hoover; he testified extensively before congressional committees as an "expert" on Communism. In his early testimony, he made the error of identifying two other FBI agents as Communists. Later, he said that he had named a thousand Party members in his sixty-three appearances as a witness. In truth, he named about three hundred persons, including several congressmen, stating that the Communists had infiltrated the Republican and Democratic parties with the goal of "gaining control of the government," and that they planned assassinations.

Although he eventually had to admit that he never saw a Communist kill anyone, he asserted that "the Communist is not only plotting murder, he's plotting mass murder. Communists plan to liquidate one third of the American population, mostly the oldsters." Moreover, the Russians had a plan to invade America via Alaska, and "all" representatives of the Soviet-bloc governments in the United Nations were spies. Cvetic's book became a radio series, and he earned sumptuously as a lecturer, while almost a hundred people in Pennsylvania lost their jobs because of his testimony. His reliability was sometimes challenged by defense lawyers because he was hospitalized three times for chronic alcoholism and once for mental illness. When his career as an agent declined, he joined the John Birch Society and claimed that "constant harassments and smears by Communists" had forced him to drink. He died of a heart attack in 1962 at the age of fifty-three, while he was taking a driving test.

Eight years after *Mission to Moscow*, the Cvetic film seems like Warner Brothers' apology for the former. One of the movie's central themes is that Communists are the true enemies of blacks, working people, and Jews. A leader says, "To bring about Communism in America, we must incite riots." Hence the Communists try to inspire blacks to assault whites—"Yes, those niggers ate it up"—and calculate that "if, after this meeting, a black goes out and kills a white man," the Party will profit on the money raised for the defense. (The movie accuses the Communists of using the Scottsboro case as a business venture, maintaining that they collected two million dollars and spent only sixty thousand dollars.) The comrades take credit for "the Negro riots" in Detroit and Harlem in 1943: "When blacks died," an FBI agent says, "they never knew that their death warrants were signed in Moscow." The Communists force a strike on the Pittsburgh steelworkers' union, and those who won't join the picket line are beaten with steel bars wrapped in *The Jewish Daily Forward,* so that Jews will be blamed for the bloodspilling. Communists also arrange devastating "accidents" at the steel plant, and then replace the badly injured workers with Party members.

Cvetic, played by Frank Lovejoy, is really a martyr for the FBI: since everyone believes him to be a Communist, his family despises him—"You slimy Red!"—and his young son gasps, "Never come near me again." He has to leave his mother's birthday party for a Communist reception where champagne is swilled while the caviar is passed, and a comrade explains, "This is how we're all going to live once we take over the country!"

"Moscow" originates a campaign to deride the House Committee on Un-American Activities in order to deceive American "suckers." "Let them howl their heads off about the rape of the First Amendment," an organizer chuckles, adding, "We need some pinko chumps!" In short, any criticism of the Committee

(OVERLEAF) *In* Trial, *directed by Mark Robson in 1955, the Communists try to exploit the case of a young Mexican-American who is wrongfully accused of murder; they want him to be judged guilty and executed so that he will be a martyr to their cause. Here, they raise money for his defense (which they plan to keep for themselves): the crowd has been asked to hold up dollar bills to form "a sea of green."*

I Was a Communist for the FBI: *the Communists provoke violence on the steelworkers' picket line. Although almost all of the plot was fictional, the movie received a nomination for an Academy Award as the best feature-length documentary of 1951.*

was dictated by the Kremlin—a theme that thunders throughout all of these movies. (In *Big Jim McLain*, where the Committee is thanked for its help in the final credits, we're told that we "owe a great debt" to the investigators—who have remained "undaunted by the vicious campaign against them.") Since the Korean War is approaching, the Communists will do their utmost to make Americans panic and lose faith in their government, as part of a program to "soften up the people." Soon, "Red riots spread from Harlem to the Battery" in protest against the trial of Communist leaders. Cvetic then testifies that the Party intends "to deliver America to Russia as a slave," and beats up the main functionary in the courthouse. The movie ends with "The Battle Hymn of the Republic" bellowing over the soundtrack, while the camera moves in for a close-up of a small bust of Lincoln.

Despite its crudities, the movie isn't comic. However, the beginning of *Walk East on Beacon* (directed by Alfred Werker) can elicit laughter from the spectators of the Eighties when the narration extols the FBI for "protecting" us—and soon we see a shot of agents opening our mail. The film is another sham-documentary, "suggested by" J. Edgar Hoover's *Crime of the Century* and "produced with the cooperation of the FBI." In 1977, I was told that the CIA was still leasing some ten prints a year from Columbia Pictures, including about five copies dubbed in foreign languages.

Such an addiction to *Walk East on Beacon* is mildly amazing because the movie, which unveils a vast network of spies in Boston, makes the Communists so incompetent that a backward child could round them up—it seems odd that the FBI had to pit its collective brain against these stumblewits. The spies hope to pirate the results of "an extraordinary scientific experiment," which involves a brilliant "new computer." (I've always yearned to watch a movie scientist working with an old computer, like a faithful retainer. But there are no old computers in Hollywood films, just as there are no old starlets.) The picture is distinguished for its one contrite Communist, who "woke up one morning and found I had a Party card," which he compares to "finding yourself married to a woman you hate"—he's promptly murdered for his infidelity—

[handwritten margin note: Cmd what about The man who walks East on Beacon holding a Reader's Digest + Pint of Milk as ID ?!]

Advertising material for Walk East on Beacon.

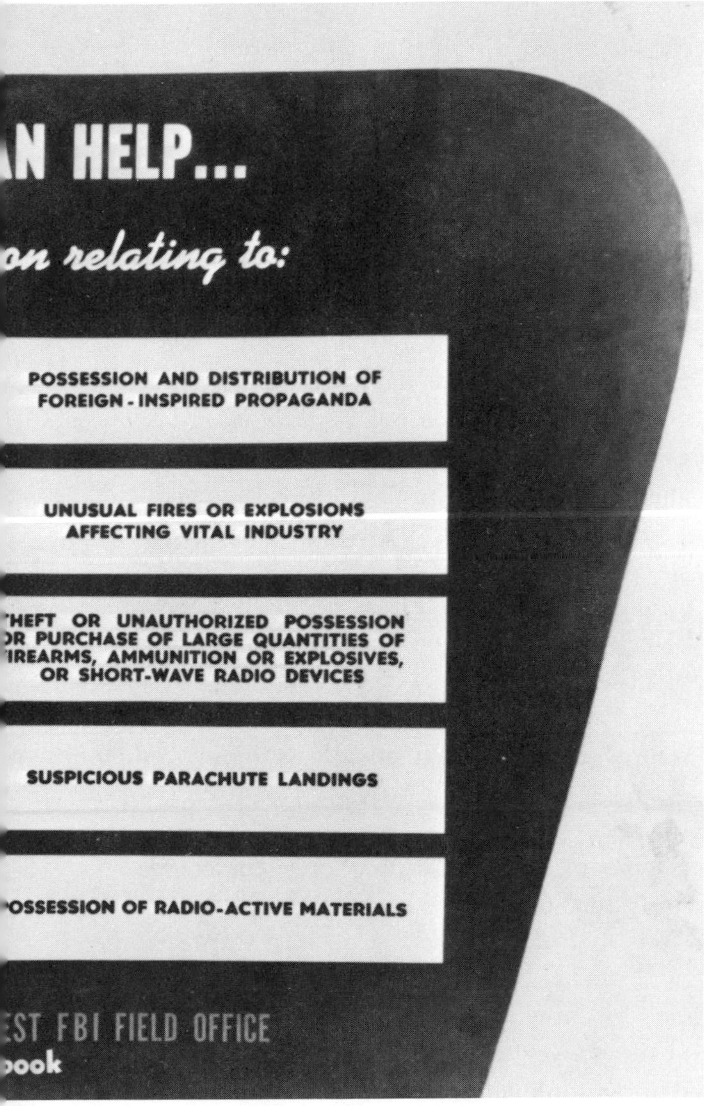

AN HELP...

on relating to:

POSSESSION AND DISTRIBUTION OF
FOREIGN - INSPIRED PROPAGANDA

UNUSUAL FIRES OR EXPLOSIONS
AFFECTING VITAL INDUSTRY

THEFT OR UNAUTHORIZED POSSESSION
OR PURCHASE OF LARGE QUANTITIES OF
FIREARMS, AMMUNITION OR EXPLOSIVES,
OR SHORT-WAVE RADIO DEVICES

SUSPICIOUS PARACHUTE LANDINGS

POSSESSION OF RADIO-ACTIVE MATERIALS

EST FBI FIELD OFFICE
book

and for the presence of George Roy Hill, a Communist who bites his pencil and resists arrest with gusto. It's exhilarating to see him struggle, shouting, "You can't pin anything on me!" but few would guess from his exertions that he would survive to direct *The World of Henry Orient* or *Butch Cassidy and the Sundance Kid* or *Slap Shot*.

•

By far the most feverish of the anti-Communist films was Leo McCarey's *My Son John*; clearly, it was made with all the sincerity that was absent in productions like *The Red Nightmare* or *I Married a Communist*. McCarey had been a particularly friendly witness before the Committee in 1947; in 1950 he had joined Cecil B. De Mille in urging all members of the Screen Directors Guild to take a loyalty oath. *My Son John* gave Helen Hayes her first starring role in seventeen years; she played the mother of Communist Robert Walker—the son whom she adores even more than her two "fighting halfbacks" in Korea, who are "fighting on God's side." As in all of the movies of this genre, the Party is the enemy of religion: Communists recoil from Christianity as the Devil does from a crucifix, and they even look uneasy when someone says, "It's time for mass."

Like so many films of the Fifties, *My Son John* focuses on the traumas of family relationships, especially the collisions between fathers and sons. But here, when it's observed that "a Communist specialty" is "breaking up homes," we're asked to side with the parents—instead of identifying with the defiant offspring, as in the James Dean movies. Hayes and her husband (Dean Jagger) are supposed to represent the humble cream of mid-America, stricken by the tragedy of having spawned a subversive son.

However, McCarey's characterizations undermine his design. The violent, threatening father—an American Legionnaire who roars that if he "thought" his son was a Communist, "I'd take you out in the backyard and give it to you with both barrels!"—and the hysterically possessive mother appear as figures from a moldy textbook on male homosexuality. One of the great moments in

Helen Hayes makes Robert Walker swear that he is not a Communist in
My Son John; as a Party member, he doesn't hesitate to lie with one hand
on the family Bible while his mother kneels at his feet.

This film is
a classic - The
others madness is so
anti-woman it stinks.
Walker's performance is
flawless.

American cinema occurs when the father hits the son on the head with the family Bible and then hurls him to his knees. (The Bible is the most important prop in this picture, as the spinning globes were in *Mission to Moscow.*) Walker's role—he's sly, furtive, flirtatious with his mother and simmering with snide hostility toward his father—is a cliché for the gay man in a period when sexual or political "deviation" were considered equally disgusting. His overconfident smile hardly ever falls out of his face, even after he camps up an ultrapatriotic song as his father clenches his fists in fury. Supercilious throughout—while even his way of smoking seems deceitful—the actor skillfully conveys that he loves his mother but also cannot stand her. Yet it's intriguing that McCarey chose such grotesque creatures as these parents for his oracles of familial and political sanity. With such a background it's no wonder that Walker ended up as a stranger on a train.

It should be remembered that the mother/son relationships in the movies of the Forties and Fifties often palpitated with a romanticism that could wring a communal shudder from the psychiatrists of today. In *Gentleman's Agreement*, Gregory Peck is totally dependent on being coached and cheered by Anne Revere; after her kiss of praise for his achievements, he sighs, "Mom, that means more than anything." In *The Pride of the Yankees*, Gary Cooper says again and again that his mother is his *"best* girl," gives her his fraternity pin, adding, "You'll have to go steady with me," and encourages her to sit on his lap. Even in *Somebody Up There Likes Me*, Paul Newman as Rocky Graziano keeps chucking his mother under the chin. While there were nagging or irksome mothers, as in *Rebel Without a Cause*, the disemboweling, all-destructive mother didn't appear until later—culminating in Angela Lansbury's role in *The Manchurian Candidate* in 1962.

Therefore, the Helen Hayes character in *My Son John* seems like an exotic mutation. Meant to be tender and gallant, whether she's clutching her adult son in a passionate embrace, singing him a frantic lullaby that he "used to love" when "I bounced you on one knee and then the other," tossing off such lines as "You were the gurglingest baby," or chewing her glove in excitement, or swallowing hard with bravery, Hayes evokes a being whom one

wouldn't want to unleash in any nursery. The film is rich in men- *yes.*
opausal warnings: her doctor repeats that "a woman at her time of
life" must beware of "strain." As she grows flustery and pitiful,
we're supposed to deduce that having a left-wing son is ravaging
her brain—however, she seemed demented from the start. The
actress is winsome between bouts of derangement, but, contrary to
the director's intentions, one could easily conclude that mothers
cause Communism.

The mother decides that her son is a Communist and therefore a spy when she has no evidence beyond her own cloudy sus-
picions. In that sense, the film mirrored the mentality of the
period—in the impulse to condemn those whose "loyalty" was in
question. When the son thinks that the mother is hiding an in-
criminating door key, and he twists her wrist while asserting that
"There are millions on our side," her clenched hand opens to
reveal a rosary: "There are millions on *my* side."

At the film's climax, Hayes spills out a torrential monologue
before Walker and an FBI agent—to whom she hopes that her son
will confess, so that she won't have to turn him in. She recalls
how she used to cheer her other sons at football—"many a game
they pulled out of the fire"—which this one never played. Stag-
gering and jerking her arms and head from side to side, she cries:
"You listen to me, John, you've got to get in *this* game, and
you've got to carry the [pause] ball yourself. . . . Take the ball,
John!" She reels about, rolling her eyes and flapping her hands.
"Time's running out. We can't stop that clock! I'm cheering for
you now!" Jumping up and down, she chants, "My son John. My-
son-John. My *son John!*" But since he doesn't admit his perfidy,
she collapses on a sofa, shouting to the FBI, "Take him away! He
has to be punished!"

Before the mother convicts her son, the movie has spelled out
the twin perils that he personifies: education and the intellect.
Hayes remarks that he's always been studious—"he has more de-
grees than a thermometer"—and that he's closer to his "highbrow
professor" than to his "low-brow" parents. The father keeps sarcastically repeating that he himself is "not bright"—thereby estab-
lishing his moral superiority to his corrupt son. Finally, it's

stressed that the son's years in college perverted his mind and sucked him into the Party.

Robert Walker died just after *My Son John* was filmed; a few of the last scenes were fleshed out with inserts from *Strangers on a Train*. His fellow Communists murder him as he speeds to purge himself before the FBI; he expires at the foot of the Lincoln Memorial. A tape recording of a commencement speech that he had planned to make at his alma mater is played to the stunned students. A heavenly ray of light grows brighter over an empty lectern as they listen to the dead man's voice delivering an awful warning to the youth of America:

"I was going to help to make a better world. I was flattered when I was immediately recognized as an intellect. I was invited to homes where only superior minds communed. It excited my freshman fancy to hear daring thoughts. . . . A bold defiance of the only authorities I'd ever known: my church and my father and mother. [His hearers' eyes widen further.] I know that many of you have experienced that stimulation. But stimulants lead to narcotics. As the seller of habit-forming dope gives the innocent their first inoculation, with a cunning worthy of a serpent, there are other snakes lying in wait to satisfy the desire of the young to give themselves to something positive. . . .

"Even now, the eyes of Soviet agents are on some of you. . . . Before I realized the enormity of the steps I had taken, I was an enemy of my country and a servant of a foreign power. . . . I am a living lie, I am a traitor, I am a native. American. Communist. Spy. And may God have mercy on my soul."

Part of the film's fascination flows from the fact that McCarey couldn't abandon the traditions of farce or the rhythm of slapstick. Even in this desperately solemn movie, the director of *Duck Soup* and *The Awful Truth* and *Going My Way* reveals himself in sudden bursts of burlesque, as when a parish priest turns playful, or when the enraged father—drunk because his wicked son has upset him—falls downstairs, sings, and falls again. Naturally, *My Son John* was meant to generate support for the Committee. But, by making a paranoid fascist of the father and a religious psychopath of the mother, the film also makes Communism sound rather tempting.

•

As the Fifties progressed, the percentage of American films that dealt with social questions continued to ebb: the studios censored themselves where even semi-political issues were concerned and, right after the 1947 investigations, the industry was so fearful about its reputation that visitors to the studios were warned not to discuss politics with anyone on the lot. Not that Hollywood had ever made many films about politics per se. But the Forties had released movies that explored poverty or free speech—or simply the difficulties of living in this country. Often, the tone was more important than the topic. Unwed mothers, tramps, prisoners who wanted to go straight, and the plight of tenant farmers and under-paid professionals had received sympathetic treatment on the screen. "But," Abraham Polonsky remembered, "after the black-list, movies were almost labeled: *Beware, do not enter this territory*—the territory was social content."

In accordance with that spirit, the producer of *Arch of Triumph* worried that there were too many references to refugees in the movie; Jack Warner cut the lines "Your father is a banker" and "My father lives over a grocery store," which were spoken by impoverished John Garfield to wealthy Joan Crawford in *Humoresque*, and the use of the word "labor" created problems in *The Treasure of the Sierra Madre*. Just as *Life* magazine was wary of "negative news"—catastrophes or injustice tended to be foreign—the studios grew more protective than ever of the national image. The tenor of the films of the Fifties was that ours was a splendid society, and that one ought to cooperate with it rather than criticize it. Still, the usual doses of violence were permissible; violence was virile, therefore healthy—just as tapdancing and Westerns and getting married had always been. And politics misted away: remote or suspect or irrelevant, they dwindled in the public consciousness, no longer a lively subject for entertainment or reflection.

IV: The Private Sector

Love, or the lack of it, the clash between generations, suburban dilemmas or sexual anxieties: these weren't unworthy themes for the major movies of a period when many were grateful to forget the war and to relax into an atmosphere where burning issues seemed to be momentarily in abeyance. However, many of the films of the Fifties were quite smotheringly introspective. As in fiction, personal relationships became far more important than public concerns—as though the two had to be mutually exclusive. Like the Broadway theater, movies focused on the rewards or miseries of intimacy, and other levels of experience were largely ignored. And the fact that most of our films, like our culture, became apolitical was a political statement in itself.

Naiveté and overstatement dominated many movies, which were drenched in floods of simplified Freudianism, and it appeared as though the wit and speed of the Thirties films had been unlearned, that the best grittiness of the social realism of the Forties was forgotten. While many fine new performers emerged, including those from the Actors Studio, their talents were often imprisoned in flaccid scripts. Censorship was probably less responsible for the decline of sophistication than the influence of tele-

101

vision. At the beginning of the Fifties, when Hollywood was forfeiting much of its audience to the small screen, producers seemed to think that movies must be made more accessible, easier to apprehend: hence the repetition of significant lines and the slowness that hadn't hampered the pictures of an earlier time.

Apparently, film makers didn't trust the spectators to grasp any situation that wasn't meticulously explained. Even so famous a property as *The Sun Also Rises* was treated as though it needed help. I read an early version of the script, which established the impotence of the hero without belaboring it (unlike the cover of the paperback edition, which proclaimed, "It was a hell of a way to be wounded!"). But while the movie was being shot, some new dialogue was inserted so that Jacob Barnes could be very carefully told what he would never be able to do again.

Meanwhile, along with the flowering of cheap science fiction, Bible epics, and magnificent musicals, many movies waded into the woes of the family. Overwhelmingly, the rebellious off-shoots condemned their parents for not loving them sufficiently, while noncommunication paralyzed all the fathers and sons who "just couldn't get through" to each other. But there was a contradiction afoot: the sons were mutinous—and yet they were clamoring for more love from their parents; instead of striking out on their own, they wanted to be closer to their families. And protest became acutely personal: it had retreated from the streets or the factories to the dining-room table and the kitchen, amid the gingham curtains and the flatware. Rarely has family life looked so repulsive as it did in the movies of a decade that also tried to uphold the family as an institution, while the parents who didn't "understand" or cherish their children were as guilty as the gangsters of a previous era.

Whether they were harsh or neglectful or merely uncomprehending, fathers did bulk large in the films of the Fifties. Parents are surely no more popular today, but the accusations are probably more varied than they were in the James Dean movies or *A Hatful of Rain* or *Tea and Sympathy*. The sons' lines ranged from "You *never* talk to me" to "Talk to me, Father!" and "I gotta talk to you," while fathers had many occasions to exclaim, "You can't talk to me like that!" (Also: "I'm at my rope's end with that boy" or "Get him out of here" and "What are children for? Why do we have them?") There was the periodic admission that "We just don't talk the same language." Moreover, a father who called his lad "a bum" was guaranteed to reduce him to emotional prostration. But daughters didn't devour much footage, unless they stayed out too late—as though the hymen might dissolve at midnight.

In a world of adults who "won't listen" to their garrulous descendants, the parents are often denounced as hypocrites, and worst of all, they're not "sincere"—a key word of the period. (In the Forties, "sincerity" sarcastically implied pretense—meaning Madison Avenue. But Hollywood drained the term of irony in the Fifties.) Sometimes insensitive fathers, who fail to dispense tenderness, wave their wallets at their embittered sons, crying, "Don't I buy you everything you want?" But a father who forgets a son's birthday can inspire a boy to behave like a nagging wife. Yet there are penitent fathers too: "There's been a long, hard silence between us." Scenes of conflict can commence with an ominous statement like "I want to be your friend, son"—along with the admission that such a project will be "difficult." And a son can deliver a lofty reproof—"Better take it easy on the bourbon, Dad"—as the father gets sloshed during their struggles at familial dialogue.

However, when love or attention aren't abundant, the sons can suddenly hate their fathers—as Anthony Franciosa did in *A Hatful of Rain* and *The Long, Hot Summer* (where he locked his father up in a burning barn), or as James Dean did in *East of Eden*—after both had been so glowingly anxious to please their exasperated begetters. Above all, not being loved ruins the character: the loveless can wax violent or go mad, or even commit

(OVERLEAF) *Orson Welles as the infuriated father of Anthony Franciosa in Martin Ritt's* The Long, Hot Summer *(1958), which was based on some stories by William Faulkner—although the movie's style was more in keeping with Tennessee Williams.*

James Dean as Raymond Massey's son in East of Eden. The movie
chastises the father for his rigid moralism, and yet he also commands the
spectators' sympathies. Massey was genuinely appalled by Dean's behavior
during the filming.

John Wayne battles with his foster son, Montgomery Clift, in Red River.

suicide, as the young Jew did in *The Dark at the Top of the Stairs.* At the very least, such deprivation stunts the growth: in *East of Eden*, Raymond Massey is told that Dean "will never be a man" unless he feels that his father loves him. Massey and Dean do finally "connect" at the movie's end—although by then, one is voiceless due to a stroke, and the other is speechless with tears.

Fathers fret—as Rock Hudson does in *Giant*—when they feel that they're losing their authority. Howard Hawks's *Red River* (1948), in which Montgomery Clift played John Wayne's adopted son, was a precursor to the generational contests of the Fifties: there, among the cattle and the cacti of the desert, the father vowed to kill the young man who had displaced him, while berating his heir for being "soft." However, a flabby father is just as threatening as a fierce one: in Nicholas Ray's *Rebel Without a Cause*, Dean is devastated by the sight of his father in an apron, carrying a tray of food to his wife's bedroom. (The son laments, "If only he had the guts to knock Mom cold, then maybe she'd be happy and stop pickin' on him.") Still, an embrace can solve everything between parent and child: all the years of mutual loathing can be erased by a prolonged manly hug.

Dean seemed dazzling in the Fifties: the face that dissolved like smoke,the body that reveled in its suppleness, the ringed eyes, sunken as a lemur's, the intensity of every gesture, every action— whether he was thrusting heads of lettuce onto a chute or chewing a sandwich, striking oil or nuzzling a milk bottle, exhorting a field of beans to grow or flinging himself down a flight of stairs. And he conveyed a febrile sexuality by appearing to be so acutely attracted to the women he wanted—especially Julie Harris. Today, his aura seems somewhat less compelling; perhaps we prefer a subtler form of narcissism in the Eighties. The mannerisms seem quite precious now, from the soupy sequences when there was too much flinching and wincing, to the habit of crouching or curling up in a foetal position—which looks just as preposterous as it did when Marlon Brando went embryonic at the end of *Last Tango in Paris.* Dean's pose of eternal suffering can grow tiresome, and so does the recurrent chuckling squeal that passed for laughter. If he'd lived, he would have acquired several pouchy chins from drawing his head into his shoulders like a man who's determined to become a turtle.

Yet all the affectations cannot hide the talent, nor the cleverness with which he was cast. Elia Kazan has called him "a pudding of hatred" and has said that Dean helped a generation to feel justified in detesting its parents. But hatred is less accurate than anger: while the silent generation was socially inhibited, there was copious wrath against the family, although few felt able to make it visible or vocal. Some psychiatrists think that Freud's popularizers confused his definition of aggression with that of hostility—hence the parents of the Thirties and Forties taught their small children to feel guilty about quite ordinary self-assertion or resentment.

Dean did personify the defiance that many subdued adolescents kept hidden. At a time when both sexes were over-awed by the period's concept of masculinity, his freedom to unfetter every emotion, to shriek or sob or thrash out conflicting feelings, was enviable as well as exhilarating. Brando's apparent virility made some young men feel inferior—he seemed to set a standard that they couldn't reach—but Dean made them feel a bit better about themselves. In the best sense, Dean was unmanly, and an adolescent girl or a young woman could identify with him, as I did.

Surely no other youthful American male was permitted so many tears onscreen as Dean was. Montgomery Clift and Anthony Perkins could be sensitive and haunted, Brando and Paul Newman could erupt with fury, but pain was Dean's province—pain without apologies, coupled with behavior that the rest of us had been schooled to control. He also seemed to have binges of exuberance with no stimulant but himself. And he *did it in public*, even in front of strangers: for us, that was almost inconceivable. As a romantic who fought for his own sanity, he also suggested that no harness could hold him—in a period when few could imagine living outside a frame.

I saw the Dean movies quite often, almost oblivious to the turgid scripts, the leaden dialogue. I cared nothing about the cult that cradled Dean; it was the mating of the actor and his roles that intrigued me, also the context. Since I was an easterner and a cultural snob, *Rebel Without a Cause* astonished me with the lavishness of technology in education and the loutishness of the students and the fact that all of them had cars. But the exoticism of California only highlighted the passions portrayed—if only more New Englanders and New Yorkers had been able to yell like that.

Still, I realized how childish *Rebel Without a Cause* was when I saw Andrzej Wajda's *Ashes and Diamonds*, made in 1958; in the Polish film, Zbigniew Cybulski's appearance and performance echoed Dean's, but the young Pole was pinioned between the deadly issues of his postwar nation, where those who had fought the Nazis then killed one another during the collision between the Communists and the Polish government in exile. Cybulski's drawn-out death from gunshot wounds near a laundry yard, where his body bled through the billowing sheets, made a mockery of Dean's anguish at being called a chicken.

•

Of course the first man whose yells rebounded in my contemporaries' consciousness was Stanley Kowalski in A *Streetcar Named Desire*—with that role, Brando seemed to give birth to a whole generation of torn T-shirts who shouted at women in white slips, while Big Daddy in *Cat on a Hot Tin Roof* was the archetypical overpowering father. But Tennessee Williams's conviction that wounded or derelict characters deserved a special sympathy was diluted in Hollywood films—to the extent that those who were pronounced "crazy" or "weird" on the screen seem quite rational today. In *Rebel Without a Cause*, Dean had to call himself "all confused" and to declare that he'd "been going around with my head in a sling for years." But, between hurricanes, he seemed to be a kindly creature, eager to "help" others, as was Brando in *On the Waterfront*, and so was Paul Newman in his early films. Why were they labeled as "anti-heroes"? Although the original Stanley Kowalski wasn't likable, the rest were amiable beings, even if they did blow fuses when outraged. And the scripts stressed that they were most often misunderstood just when they were trying to be agreeable.

Clearly, the emphasis on "craziness" reflects the period's fix-

Poster art of East of Eden: *Richard Davalos as James Dean's brother and rival for Julie Harris.*

ation on delinquents—who were laden with lines like "I'll never get close to anybody" or "Nobody can help me." *The Wild One*, for all the motorcycles and the preening in black leather, implied that the outlaws mainly needed to be given a sense of direction. But the Hollywood film makers hardly referred to the counterculture of the Fifties: they probably didn't know that it existed until Jack Kerouac's *On the Road* was published in October 1957. Rarely did a film character appear to be a "Bohemian"; there were only a few mild mavericks, such as Rock Hudson as the noble tree farmer in Douglas Sirk's *All That Heaven Allows* (1956). Hudson, whose liberated spirit is revealed by his lumberjack shirt, is given to instructing others about "freedom" from suburban conventions. As an ideal solution to the widowed Jane Wyman's loneliness, he's so rigidly polite that he emerges as a robot, even though he is capable of extracting a wine cork with his teeth.

In 1956, an obscure piece of sleaze called *The Wild Party*— which expressed contempt for squaredom and was sprinkled with such observations as "All we had was dreams, nightmares, and hi-fi," and "Man, you want to put the moon in a box"—emphasized the sinister nature of a shadowy world where those in search of "kicks" grooved on "bebop" in roadside "dives." The movie, directed by Harry Horner, is a warning to normal citizens who "crave excitement"—a craving that results in extensive knuckle-biting and violent death, which also imperiled the innocents in *The Beat Generation* (1959), where the principal hipster was a psychotic rapist. (Kerouac himself was most reasonably upset by the 1960 film of his book, *The Subterraneans*, where George Peppard played a novelist who did some spontaneous dancing to harpsichord music and captivated neurasthenic Leslie Caron by telling her, "You cook, I'll write.") Actually, Brando and Dean and the numerous delinquents were Hollywood's substitute for a counterculture, although they didn't set foot in bohemia and never pretended to be artists.

The delinquents' behavior was examined without relation to poverty, as in Richard Brooks's *The Blackboard Jungle* (1955), where fatherless wartime families were blamed for producing

[handwritten margin note: CF The odd-ball SAVAGE EYE (1960) with its Women's Eijaded View of flesh in Las Vegas]

The death of Zbigniew Cybulski in Ashes and Diamonds.

hoodlets. "Starved for affection," they took to stealing cars, working over gum machines, smoking in forbidden places, and beating up English teachers; today, we marvel at street movies bereft of drugs. The film, which opens with such nervous questions as "These kids can't be all bad, can they?" and "You don't really expect . . . trouble, do you?" prepares the spectators' glands for pandemonium: we can foresee the entire scenario after the first ten minutes. Still, some passages are distinguished by Sidney Poitier's soft-spoken insolence and the exaggerated patience with which he underlines his hostility to the white authorities: he gives one of his blackest performances as a student who trusts no one.

The movie develops into an attempt to vindicate the soft, gray English major of the Fifties (Glenn Ford, the idealistic teacher) by making him virile enough to knock down his most vicious students. A college education often depleted masculinity, as though a man's potency could be damaged by a B.A. (Here, it's obvious that Ford is an intellectual because he dines at a restaurant where Chianti bottles dangle from the ceiling.) A certain desperate liberalism hangs on the word "caring": if only responsible adults can manage to "care," then the young thugs can be tamed, and delinquency will be dissipated—once a teacher expels the two worst "influences" from his classroom. Again, personal relations outweigh social conditions, as in Don Siegel's *Crime in the Streets*, which advances the notion that adolescents "turn to crime" primarily to get attention.

The Blackboard Jungle shows a preoccupation with adults feeling of being endangered by the young. The fear of the younger generation that was common in the Sixties surfaced rather queasily in the Fifties, when therapy and sympathy were expected to solve a host of problems. In *Compulsion* (1959), Orson Welles, as a defense lawyer, speaks of a thrill-killing as "the mad act of two sick children who belong in a psychiatric hospital": the movies echoed the period's faith in psychiatry—at a time when analysts themselves were sanguine about curing almost any kind of disorder. Dutifully, the screenplays condemned delinquents while sentimentalizing them, and love persisted as an over-the-counter prescription.

In a similar vein, movies about drug addicts, such as Otto Preminger's *The Man with the Golden Arm* (1955) and Fred Zinnemann's *A Hatful of Rain* (1957), explore an individual's dependence on heroin as a personal affliction—unconnected to his surroundings. In the former, wicked beings, who happen to be pushers, victimize pure, struggling souls like Frank Sinatra, who has had "a dog's life, never a break" and a miserable marriage. (The neuroses of his clinging invalid wife are established through an image that was characteristic of the Fifties: a woman who keeps brushing her hair when she doesn't need to must be mentally unbalanced.) The movie implies that a pusher can turn someone into an addict by suggestion, merely by playing on his psyche. But such films don't admit that some addicts like to get high. The indigence of these persons isn't acknowledged—they just happen to live in battered, poorly lit buildings—although the women are beautifully coiffed, and their makeup would be suitable for Grace Kelly on a cruise. Sinatra—long-suffering and pining to go straight—is simply a sad, good man who has the misfortune to know some bad ones. Pacing the room and pounding on the walls, gulping water, shuddering and rolling on the floor and biting his wrist, the star confirms that addicts pay their dues, also that an adoring, well-groomed woman is crucial to detoxification.

We didn't see impure addicts or believable pushers until Jack Gelber's *The Connection* appeared on the stage in 1959. Sinatra's pushers wear black hombergs and checked vests; Don Murray's, in *A Hatful of Rain*, are dressed for the Ivy League, perhaps to convey their prosperity. Murray—suddenly doubled over and shivering—is more gifted than Sinatra at having the shakes. But the movie (adapted from Michael Gazzo's play, which grew out of a project at the Actors Studio) also ignores the causes of addiction. Once more, most traumas are rooted in an imperfect understanding between generations: Father (coldly): "I don't even know you."

(OVERLEAF) *Marlon Brando and his motorcycle gang in Laslo Benedek's* The Wild One. *The movie that engendered a myth did poorly when it was first released.*

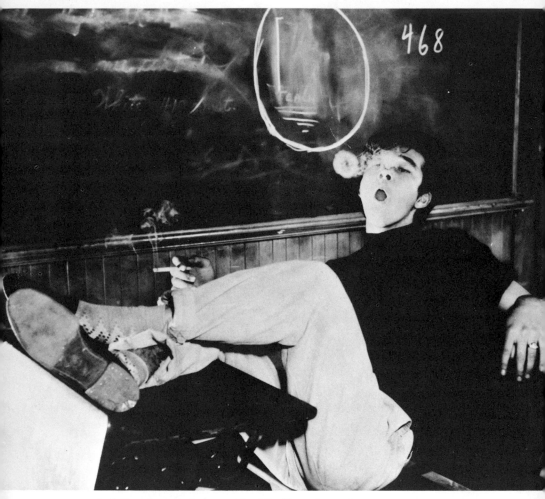

A *delinquent student in* The Blackboard Jungle.

Nasty bit of work.

Son (shrilly): "Right! You don't even know me!" It takes him an eternity to whimper, "I'm a junkie, Pop."

The exacerbations of New York are stressed—honking cars, rude taxi drivers, the grating voices of strangers in elevators, children screeching from playgrounds—but these don't seem sufficient to drive a man to the needle. And the father's dreary observation that "This is the age of the vacuum" doesn't offer many clues to a forty-dollar-a-day habit. There's an effort to use CinemaScope to emphasize the distances between those who are supposed to be close—relatives or husbands and wives—but the wide screen works against the material, since the atmosphere of a small railroad flat ought to be claustrophobic. Also, the weeping and screaming and far-flung frenzies, which were often extremely effective in the Actors Studio stage vehicles, lose their vitality in this film, where the waves of hysteria are repetitive. As in most of the pictures about delinquents, there's little sense of the slum or the ghetto; these movies could almost have been set in a Caribbean resort, and the unhappy families might as well have been on vacation.

•

While *A Hatful of Rain* did not display the influence of the Actors Studio at its best, many welcomed the impact of the Method on the movies of the Fifties. The Studio's ethos had already traveled far from its origins in Stanislavski's theories as transmitted by the Group Theatre in the Thirties. Still, the experiments in improvisation, the stress on the performer's motivations and his identification with his role, and the exercises in sense memories that can trigger stored emotions, liberated many young actors from what Elia Kazan called "the heroic, romantic, rhetorical theater."

Despite the jokes about Marlon Brando pretending to be a wax statue melting in the sun and Kim Stanley being a weeping willow, or the rumors that Lee Strasberg functioned like a psychiatrist among his students at the Studio, and complaints from playwrights that the Method actors had little respect for their words, there was no question that movies were enriched by the techniques of unlocking interior passions which the Strasberg disciples had

learned. In fact, Strasberg's lessons were probably a better prepa-
ration for screen acting than for the stage; since he urged actors to
draw on their own characters and their intimate experience, some
developed personae of the magnitude that Hollywood required.
Certain critics thought that most never strayed far enough from
themselves, or that they failed to invent new selves, but autobio-
graphical acting was hardly a sin in Hollywood.

In the theater, the Method actors could and did mangle Che-
kov, because they often threw the lines away. But since movies
aren't literary, the anti-verbal approach was appropriate to the fu-
rious dislocation that was one of the themes of the time. Also,
since they had been taught to be so aware of the facial muscles,
the close-up served them very well: the slightest wince or the fleet-
ing frown that was lost on stage was caught by the camera, as were
the small gestures that couldn't have been detected by a Broadway
audience. And muttered exclamations could be recorded to convey
the feelings that the actors disdained to enunciate. Moreover, the
"private moment" which was practiced at the Studio—when performers strove to behave in public as they did in solitude—could
be even more incisive when it was augmented by the screen.

Some felt that the Studio's style did not range beyond inarti-
culation, but that wasn't accurate: although Brando was expert at
throttling his thoughts, Eli Wallach's ingenious Sicilian in *Baby
Doll* was one of the most eloquent performances of the period,
while Ben Gazzara as a sadistic military cadet in *The Strange One*
and Paul Newman as a suspected barn-burner in *The Long, Hot
Summer* didn't fumble the lines that they hurled at their antagonists. Most of all, the Studio's training enhanced the immediacy
of males in revolt against the blandness or the hypocrisy of their
backgrounds: the crash of a fist against a door or the howl of in-
dignation or the blazing eyes had an authenticity that even the
meekest spectators could savor.

•

Meanwhile, husbands and wives asked one another the question
that also bedecked Broadway in the Fifties: "Why don't we touch

any more?" The psychic wound had replaced economic anxiety on the screen, and withholding love was much worse than withholding a paycheck. "Touching" meant "communication" as well as sex: "Sometimes you seem so far away from me" would reap the tired reply, "I'm not, darling, really." There are many references to the fact that "the music's stopped," and in a tuneless marriage it's horribly significant when husbands forget to tell their wives that they're "still pretty." Yet most couples feel that they "ought to be" happy—and wonder why they're not. At the end of the decade Arthur Miller spoke about "the romantic neuroticism" of "the theater of the blues," where "all conflict tends to be transformed into sexual conflict"—a trend that was even more conspicuous in the movies than on the stage.

From *The Catered Affair* and *The Dark at the Top of the Stairs* to *No Down Payment* and *The Man in the Gray Flannel Suit*, emotional deprivation was the groundnote of the period, and so was the need to be needed. Not letting someone "need" you amounts to neglect. Wives say, "Why don't you let me love you?" or "I want to help you but I don't know how." Perhaps the loudest aria of neediness was Fred Zinnemann's *The Men* (1950), where Brando, as a paraplegic veteran, resented Teresa Wright's cloying insistence that both of them "needed" to "help" each other. (Whether he was a baleful cripple or a Mexican revolutionary, Brando always excelled at rebuffing women.)

The heroes may keep their women at a distance—"You seem to hold yourself aloof from me"—and it was sometimes a sign of strength not to be too "involved" with females. The remote man had previously belonged to the frontier tradition, to the Western; in the Fifties, he settled in the suburbs, where he often preferred

(OVERLEAF) *As Hollywood was losing its audience to the small screen in the Fifties, film makers constantly derided television, which was accused of rinsing the soul out of family life; in Nunnally Johnson's* The Man in the Gray Flannel Suit, *Gregory Peck returns from a demanding day at the office to find that his addicted children have no time or words for him.*

a sip of his Sunday martini to his wife's kiss. The helpmate's experience of rejection could swiftly lead to accusations of fatigue ("You can't mean that—you must be tired"), which usually climaxed in a marital brawl: confrontation in the patio, or fury in the breakfast nook. At the peak of a battle, it was customary to cry out, "Why do we do this to each other?" or "What's the matter with us?"

Suburban suffering was very popular on the screen; in a world where husbands ask one another's permission to dance with their wives, and private lives are led in public—couples fight during backyard barbecue parties where everyone hears and stares—we're soberly informed that security generates restlessness. A young woman who complains that she "has nothing to do" is urged to "develop a hobby"; when she retorts that she wants to have a baby, she's warned to wait until her husband receives a promotion. (Although these films harp on "affluence" and the characters own all the latest appliances, they keep worrying about money—as though the screenwriters could never forget the Depression.) A man who deplores the weekly pot roast on the night that his child gets mumps and the refrigerator breaks down suddenly discovers that he's "outgrown" his wife. In short, many quite ordinary movies of the Fifties did raise valid questions about the constrictions of middle-class American life—which were then hastily resolved by pregnancy or an increase in salary: almost any problem could be banished by the advent of embryos or dollars.

At the same time, there was a fascination with adultery, even if it wasn't consummated. But often death was preferable to divorce: the abrupt, unexpected demise of a ghastly spouse (like Sinatra's in *The Man with the Golden Arm*) permitted transports that wouldn't otherwise have been possible. In *A Hatful of Rain*, the wife is relieved to learn that her husband is an addict—when she had feared that he was "seeing" another woman; in that movie, infidelity is worse than heroin. If many marriages were monstrous—and numerous movies said that they were—the mismatched couples were usually supposed to cleave together at all costs, to "work on" their blighted relationships. People who need each other as much as they need leprosy make remarks like "All we've got is each other" and then pledge themselves to dismal reconciliations; there are happy endings for thoroughly incompatible persons.

Loneliness was another preoccupation of the decade, when the film personae often told each other, "You don't know what loneliness is"—or what solitude "means." In Delbert Mann's *Marty*, the stress on physical unattractiveness nearly doomed Ernest Borgnine and Betsy Blair to lifetimes of isolation—until desolation forced both to accept the other's flaws. But since love was the remedy for almost everything from homicidal tendencies to overweight or schizophrenia, love began to sound medicinal—or like an investment. The period was short on genuine romance— there were no movies on a par with *Casablanca*—but love was a currency that Americans owed to one another, unless they had been mated by James M. Cain or Alfred Hitchcock. However, the pictures of the Fifties punished those who were "incapable" of love, like Anne Baxter in *All About Eve* or Kim Stanley in *The Goddess* and Andy Griffith in *A Face in the Crowd*. After the inevitable scene of denunciation, there's rarely any salvation for those who are told that they "can't love" anyone; soon their careers are likely to collapse, or their cars skid off bridges, or their closest relatives walk out on them.

Usually sex was disguised as love to a degree that wasn't totally required by the Production Code: a steamy scene was often larded with declarations of devotion between those who'd never kissed before; the very first embrace propelled discussions of marriage, and simple randiness implied commitment. Many films of the Thirties and Forties had been more worldly in this realm. But

(OVERLEAF) *The claustrophobia of family life and a debilitating marriage: Debbie Reynolds, Ernest Borgnine, and Bette Davis in Richard Brooks's* The Catered Affair (1956), *where a threadbare couple may invest much more than they can afford in their daughter's wedding. The parents fear that if they don't spend a lot of money, others will think that they are poor—an anxiety of the Fifties.*

marriage was wedded to love in the Fifties, when heroines like Joanne Woodward in *The Long, Hot Summer* were instructed that "A woman's only half a thing without a man."

In *A Place in the Sun,* Montgomery Clift passionately conveys his desire for Elizabeth Taylor, but he has to wrestle with some painfully soggy lines immediately after the initial clinch. The movie deliberately robs Theodore Dreiser's *An American Tragedy* of almost any social analysis; the fact that Dreiser became a Communist a few months before his death in 1945 made the studio executives extremely apprehensive about approaching his work in 1950, and Paramount made director George Stevens water down the first version of the script. Specifically, he had to trim the implication that the hero was a victim of the system and to inflate the love story. (Later, after Anne Revere was blacklisted, most of her major scenes were cut.) But despite the defanging of Dreiser, Clift's performance as the outsider outstrips most of the other exercises in alienation that were prevalent then, and Shelley Winters's dilating desperation makes even her timidity very threatening.

In Fred Zinnemann's *From Here to Eternity,* the legendary beach scenes between Deborah Kerr and Burt Lancaster were considered racy in 1953. But the shots of breaking waves and torrential spray—as a metaphor for sex—tend to convulse spectators of the Eighties: each time the ocean roars, so does the audience. When Kerr clasps her lover, the camera dutifully returns to the wedding ring on her finger, but her adulterous ecstasies are partially excused because her husband was "cheating" on her with "a hatcheck girl" when she was in labor—it was his fault that their baby was born dead. Soon after their sandy exertions, Kerr and Lancaster vow to marry. But an illicit pair still had to suffer when enraptured: "I've never been so miserable in my life as I've been since I met you." "Neither have I." "I wouldn't trade a minute of it." "Neither would I."

Sexual frustration was also featured throughout the decade; from many American movies, one might conclude that few had any satisfaction in the sack. The married suffer most, as Elizabeth

Even here, Prewitt doesn't buck the "system"—he bucks the bad apples in it—Holmes + his boxing gorillas / Privatization of conflict again—not to mention the gutting of the whole stockade—IWW, etc sequence from the novel. pacifism

The exasperations of suburban marriage: Cameron Mitchell and Joanne Woodward in Martin Ritt's No Down Payment *(1957).*

Taylor did in *Cat on a Hot Tin Roof,* or Anna Magnani in *Wild Is the Wind.* But even young women who guard their virginity as though it were a stock certificate—like Natalie Wood in *Marjorie Morningstar*—are permitted a fair degree of stalled sexuality. Deprived of sex, women become "nervous"; being "thwarted" can result in religious mania, as it did for Kim Stanley's mother in *The Goddess.* One may be grateful that female sexuality was acknowledged at all, but the notion that raging hormones could ravage a woman's brain was quite overpowering. In that respect, Elia Kazan's *Splendor in the Grass* is typical of the Fifties, even though it was made in 1961; Natalie Wood went out of her mind because she remained intact.

Yet most of the Fifties films still insist that a woman who refuses to slide between the sheets is the most desirable. Heroes had to plump for chastity: in *Love in the Afternoon,* Gary Cooper muses, "A girl may look as pure as freshly fallen snow—and then you find the footprints of a hundred men." Halfway decent creatures who do succumb deliver an obligatory line like, "You probably think I'm a tramp." However, in B-pictures like *The Next Voice You Hear . . . ,* even a woman picked up in a bar looks so presentable that she might be a buyer at Bergdorf Goodman.

Nymphomania was toyed with, but not flaunted; "oversexed" women, like Carroll Baker, could be identified by their excellent posture: they always thrust their shoulders back, and some owed their physical fitness to jitterbugging in "juke joints," among the pinball machines. (Jazz or early rock were often associated with depravity; unbridled music meant unbridled sex.) Costume automatically determined a woman's character, and the enticing women who gave men "the wrong idea" were constantly reprimanded for their wardrobes. A teacher who was almost raped by a delinquent in *The Blackboard Jungle* should not have worn "flesh-colored" stockings, Lee Remick was guilty of eschewing a girdle in *Anatomy of a Murder,* where the tightness of her clothing and the bareness of her legs were lengthily discussed, and Joanne Woodward was berated for her "revealing" backless dress in *No Down Payment.* Really cheap women had to have rigid permanents—sexuality wasn't yet symbolized by long, loose hair; they handled their fur stoles with abandon, and were unreasonably impatient in traffic jams, honking their horns in loud futility. The highest heels indicated a lapse in morals, and when a garishly dressed woman says to a man, "Can I talk to you for a moment?," we know that she's pregnant.

While Marilyn Monroe was a fantasy figure, the young actresses who were cast in traditional roles were usually required to be ladies. Joanne Woodward was one of the few who were allowed to be raucous (in *No Down Payment* and *The Three Faces of Eve*) as well as refined (in *The Long, Hot Summer* and *The Three Faces of Eve*). In her best parts, she was able to play the kind of spirited woman who was scarce on the screen in the Fifties: a person who won't be bullied. Lee Remick—who exuded intelligence even though she was often assigned to brainless roles—sometimes had the manic charm of a being with far more energy than her leisurely life could employ. Characterized as "a wellborn wanton," she appeared in many provocative parts, but she had a species of grace that dignified her sexy carelessness. Julie Harris, who evoked acumen and a privileged sensibility, was limited to fey or rather passive roles—as in *East of Eden*, where her character didn't develop beyond the capacity of a comforter. Yet even a lady could be derided for her virtues: a boorish man may tell an articulate woman that she reminds him of a teacher or a governess—meaning a permanent spinster.

Opportunities for the talents of Woodward, Remick, and Harris didn't equal those that flourished for the two most emblematic actresses of the period: Grace Kelly and Audrey Hepburn. Kelly's lofty perfections, the cool white hand on the fevered male brow, the intimation that a subtle sensuality might lurk beneath the lacquered exterior, enabled her to be occasionally diverting—as when she was directed by Alfred Hitchcock. Otherwise, she was formidably genteel: even her profile implied reproof.

Meanwhile, many adolescent girls of the Fifties were almost tyrannized by the image of Audrey Hepburn: hers was the manner by which ours was measured, and we were expected to identify with her, or to use her as a model. Some young women did imitate the downcast eyes, the whispery voice, the wistful poise, and the vulnerability that was worn like an expensive garment. Even more of a lady than Kelly, Hepburn blended cuteness and elegance with a sham innocence that almost insulted human nature. The innocence seemed false because no one over fifteen could have remained so sheltered as her screen personae—not even in the Fifties. Arch as well as winsome, she often wore little white gloves—even as the Bird Girl in *Green Mansions,* she conveyed a well-gloved mentality.

Had she been a better actress, her style would not have been oppressive. But her ability was meager: beyond batting her eyelids with regal authority or dispensing sudden grins and bursts of over-animation—to show that even a princess could unbend—she didn't exert herself at acting; rather, she loaned her presence to movies that relied on the responses of durable men like Gregory Peck and William Holden to an adorable child in couture clothing. (Leslie Caron, appearing in similar roles, emerged as a much more inventive performer, and exhibited an amusing resilience even in films like *Gigi.*) Flirtatious yet almost sexless, Hepburn appealed because she was utterly unmenacing to men. The running joke of *Breakfast at Tiffany's* was the notion that she would have a number of lovers. She also had a helpless, martyred quality, even when she was revealed in a new gown by Givenchy: again, a victim couldn't be a threat. All in all, the public's adulation of Hepburn seemed to tell us that young women ought to be well-heeled, submissive, and sexually spotless—sophisticated at parties, perhaps, but free of genital vibrations.

•

Outside of Westerns and conventional gangster pictures, the leading roles for the male stars of the mid-Fifties were apt to be delinquents or professionals, such as businessmen or lawyers; for the most prominent actors, there was a choice between black leather or gray flannel. (Movie scientists, garbed in crisp white coats while they held test tubes up to the light, were rare in serious produc-

Billy Wilder's The Apartment (1960): Shirley MacLaine was a
transitional woman in the Fifties—although childlike, she was earthy, and
a durable self-mockery kept her persona afloat.

tions: most were exiled to science fiction.) Men could be rugged or respectable, but few—apart from Spencer Tracy—managed to be both.

Businessmen had often been felons in the films of the Thirties and Forties; the Depression mentality had lingered until after the war. In prewar comedies like Frank Capra's, tycoons exploited "the little people," as they were called—when the wicked capitalists gathered, their snowy shirtfronts gleamed evilly beneath the chandeliers and among the candelabra, and it was almost fatal to trust anyone who had a bank account. But after the House Committee on Un-American Activities had disciplined Hollywood, and Ayn Rand had decried the image of industrialists as "crooks" and "chiselers," no American movie was going to suggest that business was unchaste.

Yet even at the height of that circumspect time, some quite conventional movies did impart a distinct alarm about what happened to men in the corporate world. Robert Wise's *Executive Suite* (1954) and Nunnally Johnson's *The Man in the Gray Flannel Suit* (1956) and Fielder Cook's *Patterns* (1956) all stated that men could be demoralized by their jobs. These particular melodramas are livelier than some of their predecessors of the Forties: the tempo is rapid, and the films are surprisingly entertaining for standard Hollywood products. It's also striking that these movies express so much confidence in the economy; they mirror the mood of the prosperous Fifties, when our institutions were celebrating the consumer society.

But although business is blooming, the films are rife with coronaries: the scripts dwell on the high price of success on Wall Street or Madison Avenue, which can ruin a man's health, destroy his relationship with his family, and even kill him. In *Executive Suite*, William Holden says, "I'm not going to *die young* at the *top of the tower*," and Barbara Stanwyck, whose lover collapses

←

Grace Kelly is courted by Alec Guinness in Charles Vidor's The Swan.

Audrey Hepburn being poignant in Billy Wilder's Sabrina *(1954).*

from strain, sighs, "What did I ever get out of the company—except loneliness and sudden death?"

Since a man's work can be lethal, a truly devoted wife (like June Allyson) doesn't want him to be promoted—whereas a disloyal woman demands that he rise in the firm. But any husband is prone to repeat to his wife that "some day" he'll make her "proud," and she almost has to reply that she "believes" in him. Few women appear in these movies: there are only the supportive spouses or the greedy, materialistic wives, and executive secretaries who are secretly in love with their employers. Sometimes the junior secretaries gossip around the coffee wagon about the men's triumphs; if sequels had been made in the Seventies, they would have been full of affirmative action suits.

The attitude toward money in these pictures wasn't romantic—as it was in most Hollywood films. Here, riches didn't mean yachts or pools or vast estates or glamour, but austere leather upholstery and perhaps fine cigars. A man who receives a major promotion will be given a rubber plant all his own. Discretion and decorum are the trappings of genuine power; the gifted financier is not vulgar about money, and he never discusses it in public.

Instead, the focus is on advancement—and the enterprising hero may come to doubt that he wants to be elevated after all. In the Fifties, ambition was not admired or even approved of; the buried anti-Semitism of the period is reflected in these movies, along with the Ivy League's suspicion that hustling was Jewish— no one wanted to be called "an operator." All the men in these films are Wasps, and their aspirations are tactfully examined. (Unlike Tony Curtis in *Sweet Smell of Success*, they couldn't declare that "I'm nice to people when it pays me to be nice!" or wallow in their puissance like Burt Lancaster.) No script hints that they might be happier if they were self-employed, or if they functioned outside the marketplace.

While the intricate strategies and tactics of office life are dramatized, it's difficult for the gentlemanly heroes in narrow lapels to plot with others, or to challenge the bosses' ideas. They look uncomfortable at board meetings, amid all the crackling of thick

[handwritten marginal note: big difference today?]

papers and the significant glances cast at secret ballots. Clearly, it's harrowing for nice, upright men like Holden or Gregory Peck or Van Heflin to step out of line, to be assertive or aggressive. And in *The Man in the Gray Flannel Suit*, when Peck turns down an excellent assignment so that he can spend more time with his family, his kindly employer praises him for his priorities.

And yet the leading men of the Fifties couldn't appear to be infirm. Therefore, when they convince themselves that they should try to move upward, they announce that "It's for the good of the company"—to which they are always faithful, even though they suffer on its premises. Thus, the heroes are presented as men of conscience who ascend on their own merits—a fond fantasy of Hollywood. Meanwhile, their opponents indulge in naked, searing competition: to obtain a raise from seven thousand to nine thousand dollars a year. Most bosses are benign—with the exception of sadistic Everett Sloane in *Patterns*, who snarls that his firm "can't be run like a welfare comfort station"—but there's often one executive who specializes in humiliating others.

Men who are depressed by their jobs may go on binges; the next day's hangover reveals an extraordinary amount of stubble on the chin—as though whiskey were a hair stimulant. (Still, few abandon propriety: in *Executive Suite*, an employee without a tie is sharply ordered to "get dressed.") But while these movies show that success in "the chromium jungle" is extremely dangerous to respiration or circulation, and very damaging to home life, they hardly criticize the system. Severe problems at the office are usually caused by one very unpleasant individual; when his schemes are defeated, all will be well. As in *The Blackboard Jungle*, the issues are reduced to the level of personal conflict or behavior. Yet the passions that these films display belie the optimistic endings: despite the colleagues' congratulations and the beaming wife, we sense that heart attacks await those who are full of brave resolve to improve the company or its performance.

•

There were notably few comedies in the Fifties, and the occasional farces, such as the labored *The Seven Year Itch* and the sublime

Some Like It Hot—both directed by Billy Wilder—shrank from subtlety. Joseph Mankiewicz's *All About Eve,* one of the few really *written* movies of the period, was a time-traveler: the style of rapid riposte and jubilant wisecrack belonged to the Thirties. Screen comedies thrived during the Depression due to the very harshness of the era, which augmented the public's appetite for amusement, for laughter as an engine of survival. But in the Fifties survival was hardly at stake.

For all its durable charms, *All About Eve* is rather unsettling today because it so sternly rebukes women for being ambitious—which means that Bette Davis and Anne Baxter must also be seething neurotics. (Gloria Swanson in *Sunset Boulevard* and Kim Stanley in *The Goddess* were equally tainted.) In *All About Eve,* the cast keeps remarking that Davis is terribly difficult—although she doesn't seem so to a contemporary audience. After all, the script makes her very likable indeed. The film leans heavily on her age (forty) and the notion that she can't be a "real woman" unless she has a husband: being a successful actress does not justify her existence.

When one sees *All About Eve* now, it's clear that two of the characters should have been gay: George Sanders as the suave, venomous theater critic (undoubtedly drawn from Alexander Woollcott and George Jean Nathan), and Eve herself. Anne Baxter's ardent infatuation with Davis seems thoroughly lesbian. If the sexes were reversed in this movie, imagine a film of 1950 that dared to portray such a relationship between a famous male actor and a worshipful young man—which would have been unthinkable. It's also unconvincing when Sanders asserts that Eve "belongs" to him, or that sex occurred between them: the idea that he would find her physically attractive isn't faintly believable. Baxter was an odd choice for an impassioned individual or a talented actress—her manner is too throaty and dewy, even for a hypo-

(OVERLEAF) *Everett Sloane, Van Heflin, and several other businessmen witness a colleague's heart attack in* Patterns.

George Sanders and Anne Baxter in All About Eve.

Gloves <u>and</u> a cigarette
holder — no yellow stain
for G.S.

crite—and yet she could be a sexual confidence-woman: a gay person who sometimes pretends to be straight.

The Motion Picture Code forbade the depiction of homosexuality; the word "pansy" couldn't be uttered on the screen, and it's rather amazing that Robert Walker was able to play his particular roles in *Strangers on a Train* and *My Son John*. (Still, in each case, the effeminate man was a villain.) The Code began to ease its strictures in 1962. But from the perspective of the Eighties, it's easy to see which movie characters should have been gay in the Fifties, such as Sal Mineo in *Rebel Without a Cause*—where his adoration of James Dean illustrates the period's uneasy fascination with "latency." Since that was such a fashionable concept, some pundits presumed that the bonded males in *Marty* were repressed homosexuals—an interpretation that Paddy Chayefsky rejected with gusto.

The homosexual themes were purged from the movie versions of *A Streetcar Named Desire* and *Cat on a Hot Tin Roof.* (The films of plays were so often inferior to what had been staged because movie scripts were crammed with the clichés of compromise and explanation.) In the meantime, popular legend alleged that James Dean and Marlon Brando and Cary Grant and Montgomery Clift were bisexual; it was rumored that Sal Mineo was gay. Hence the image of the American male hero was tinged with perplexity: if those stars preferred their own sex, then sexual deception seemed more necessary than ever, and it was crucial to pretend that homosexuality did not exist.

Throughout *Compulsion*, which was adapted from the Leopold and Loeb case, the word "homosexual" is never used, although the young murderers are made to giggle abundantly and to be "very careful about" their clothes. One talks to his teddy bear, while the other is considered "strange" because he's an ornithologist; it's repeated that they have "no girls." Finally, they're identified as "powder puffs" and "dirty little degenerates." Director

(OVERLEAF) *Deborah Kerr and John Kerr in* Tea and Sympathy.

Richard Fleischer thought his film outspoken and said that Alfred Hitchcock's *Rope*, which was based on the same case, had "skirted the issue." *Compulsion* dwells on the killers' "superior intellects" and implies that such "brilliance" can warp the moral sense: the idea that scholarship is "unnatural" is pungent in this movie. However, the character who really deserved to be gay was the boy in Vincente Minnelli's *Tea and Sympathy.*

Some of us who saw the play on Broadway when we were students felt that it insulted us—by suggesting that our generation could be so naive about sex. The stage hit made a truly embarrassing movie: one squirms in the darkness at what passed for "maturity." John Kerr's hearty, back-slapping father, who recoils from his son's kiss of greeting and objects to the boy planting flowers, cooking, sewing on buttons, and folksinging—activities that were even more damning than the bird-watching in *Compulsion*—recalls that when they last tried to have "a heart-to-heart talk," the son threw up. It's plain that listening to classical music signifies misery and defeat, and when Kerr's style of walking is criticized as "light," we realize that the boys in the film were supposed to walk as though they were wearing jockstraps.

Kerr moons over Deborah Kerr—unhappily married to his housemaster—who finally has sex with him to prove that he isn't homosexual. The movie alters the play's ending: on Broadway, she slowly unbuttoned her blouse while enunciating, "Years from now . . . when you talk about this . . . and you will . . . be kind"— a line that became a camp joke in the Fifties. (It was almost as famous as one of the crowning lines of *Rebecca:* "That's not the Northern Lights, that's Manderley!") Before *Tea and Sympathy* was filmed, a group of seventeen Catholic bishops declared that adultery must not be condoned: hence Deborah Kerr had to suffer and repent at the conclusion. The Legion of Decency suggested that she ought to die after she was divorced, but her survival was permitted.

On screen, both Kerrs are dreadfully awkward, especially together. With almost every gesture, the actor tries to tell the audience that he's normal; he's stolid when he's meant to be sensitive, and he expresses his longing for her by raising his shoulders to-ward his ears and pulling in his chin. Deborah Kerr pipes out golden platitudes in a high, didactic voice; when distressed, she swallows delicately, while he swallows tearfully—in fact, I've not seen so much swallowing in any movie.

The message of *Tea and Sympathy*—that it's all too easy to smear someone—is awash with liberal intentions, and the script chides those who think that the boy is homosexual. The stress is on the horrors of injustice—toward someone who's not culpable as charged. (Naturally, the abuse of real homosexuals isn't an is-sue.) The film states that it would be catastrophic to be gay, and the text seems like a heterosexual reproof to Tennessee Williams and William Inge. *Tea and Sympathy* also seems anti-female: it evokes the all-understanding woman as suffocating and over-pro-tective, and she seems quite castrating to us today. On stage, she was bathed in light like a madonna; in the movie, she's even more engulfing. The film extinguished the play's few nuances, and the ending was almost an apology for sex. As in most of the movies of the period, passion was tagged with a penalty: Hollywood couldn't let us take it lightly.

V: Behind the Waterfront

Amid the waving tentacles from outer space and the lamentable family relationships and the CinemaScopic lunges at the Bible, *On the Waterfront* was a milestone that measured the distance between the radicalism of the Thirties and the recantations of the Cold War—as well as one of the most provocative movies of any period. The chasm between its conception and the final product symbolizes the conflicts among those who were re-examining their participation in American history. Directed by Elia Kazan and written by Budd Schulberg, released in 1954, *On the Waterfront* attempted to vindicate the cooperative witness who named names—as Schulberg did in 1951 and Kazan did in 1952, when each appeared before the House Committee on Un-American Activities. But the original idea was Arthur Miller's—who refused to identify Communists to the Committee in 1956. Kazan and Schulberg had been Party members for a short time in the Thirties; Miller had not.

After the stage success of *Death of a Salesman* in 1949, Miller spent many hours bicycling around Brooklyn, where he lived. In Red Hook, he noticed a question chalked all over pavements and walls and the sides of trucks: "DOVE PETE PANTO?"— Where is Pete Panto? Curious about the source of the graffiti,

Miller queried men in neighborhood bars, but no one wanted to answer him.

Eventually he learned that Pete Panto was a young longshoreman who had tried to organize a protest in his local unit of the International Longshoremen's Association against the gangsters who controlled the harbor. As Miller wrote in 1975, "Pete Panto was sleeping in cement at the bottom of the river": he had been murdered by the mob, hence almost everyone who knew the facts was afraid to talk.

Miller wrote a screenplay based on the case, titled *The Hook*, and he and Kazan—who had directed *Death of a Salesman*—offered the script to Harry Cohn, the president of Columbia Pictures. Cohn, who had been decorated by Mussolini after producing an admiring short about the dictator in 1933, was wary; he didn't like the script, but he agreed to finance it—in hope that Kazan would later direct a more commercial movie for him. Kazan was then the most exalted director on Broadway: he had already directed Thornton Wilder's *The Skin of Our Teeth*, S.N. Behrman's *Jacobowsky and the Colonel*, Tennessee Williams's *A Streetcar Named Desire*, and many others, including Miller's *All My Sons*. At the peak of his powers, Kazan incited numerous performers to levels of passion that yielded the finest acting of their careers; he was responsible for the most exciting productions of the postwar theater, and Marlon Brando and James Dean would soon owe their eminence to working with him.

Since Miller's waterfront script focused on a union, Cohn showed it to Roy Brewer, the chairman of the AFL Film Council and the most powerful unionist in Hollywood, where he was also known as "the toughest anti-Communist in town"; he had testified against many alleged culprits. Brewer was particularly vigilant about the content of films: in 1947, he told the Committee that the Communists were trying to "control the unions" in order to tyrannize the producers and then to "force their ideas" into movie scripts. He complained that the writers of the Left had injected movies with "poverty, corruption, injustice, bigotry, and discrimination. They downgraded patriotism and religion in American life." In 1961, he wrote in *The American Legion* magazine that the Communists had "urged" writers "to march on picket lines and otherwise taste the sordid side of life. Out of this came a tendency toward stories dealing with violence, sex, divorce, prostitution, and miscegenation. Pictures began to make heroes and sympathetic characters out of persons who were outside the pale of social acceptability."

Harry Cohn informed Miller that if Brewer vetoed the script, no Columbia movie could be shown by any union projectionist throughout this country. Not long after, Brewer told Miller that the screenplay was "a lie"—since no AFL union would traffic with criminals, especially not the Longshoremen's. (Joseph Ryan, the president of the International Longshoremen's Association, was a long-term friend of Brewer's; Ryan finally had to leave his post after the State Crime Commission established the union's affiliation with racketeers, and he was also convicted of grand larceny.) But a few years before the impurities of Ryan's union were exposed, Brewer told Miller that no loyal American could have written such a script—and that a movie of that nature would inspire "turmoil" on the New York docks, where the supplies for our troops in Korea were being handled.

Brewer added that he had found the screenplay so appalling that he had passed it on to the local FBI—so that the staff could speculate on the amount of disruption that such a movie might generate on the waterfront. Soon Miller was instructed that "all" he "had to do" was to rewrite the story—"so that instead of racketeers terrorizing the dockworkers, it would be the Communists." (*I Married a Communist*, also known as *The Woman on Pier 13*, had already used that scenario, but there the villain was meant to suggest Harry Bridges, who had actually ejected the gangsters from his branch of the International Longshoremen's and Warehousemen's Union—which had been formed after Ryan discharged Bridges from the ILA.)

Miller replied that he knew that there were Communists working on the waterfront—two of them. He was acquainted with both men. He argued that to multiply their numbers into hundreds, and to exaggerate their influence, would make the criminals appear as patriots. So he cancelled the whole project. Cohn cabled him promptly: "STRANGE HOW THE MINUTE WE WANT TO MAKE THE SCRIPT PRO-AMERICAN MILLER PULLS OUT."

•

Other vehicles for Kazan's energies were abundant. *Viva Zapata!* was made shortly before he testified; in his statement to the Committee, Kazan claimed that his movie about the Mexican revolutionary was "an anti-Communist picture." He has since called it "progressive." The film's highly confused romanticism did invite conflicting interpretations: *The Daily Worker* defined it as "Trotskyist," Samuel Fuller said that an idealist had been turned into a murderer, and Howard Hawks complained that "a disgusting bandit" had been converted into "a Santa Claus." Adrian Scott of the Hollywood Ten wrote that its "theme" was that "power corrupts revolutionaries." Brando's rather oriental makeup and his dead-end New York accent defused the supposition that he was a Mexican peasant, while Anthony Quinn, as Brando's brother, appeared to be auditioning for *Zorba the Greek* more than a decade in advance, and much of the cast seemed committed to Yiddish theater.

Kazan said that the Communists were angered because John Steinbeck's script emphasized that Zapata had "turned his back on power" at the height of victory; the director reasoned that his opponents felt that he had vitiated the strength of a left-wing hero. However, the political intentions of the movie are obscured by its lumbering extravagance and the lineaments of a rousing action film. Kazan's next project, *Man on a Tightrope* (1953), was a routine Iron Curtain picture that followed a circus troop escaping from Czechoslovakia; like *Viva Zapata!* the movie succeeded only during its crowd scenes, where Kazan's unique talents for orchestrating masses of bodies outshone the weakness of his casting.

On the Waterfront was reborn in the early Fifties, when Kazan invited Schulberg to work with him on a movie that would be filmed in the East. They researched the harbor, and Schulberg wrote a script—based on a series of Pulitzer prize-winning articles by Malcolm Johnson in *The New York Sun*—which was rejected by every studio in Hollywood: none thought that it would be profitable. Finally, Sam Spiegel became the independent producer, and the movie was shot in Hoboken, New Jersey. And when some radicals and liberals objected to *On the Waterfront* as an anti-union film made by two political informers, few knew that the movie was first conceived by a man who never contributed a name to the Committee, but who had felt compelled to express what he knew about crime on the New York docks. (Miller did not feel that his material had been lifted, since his script "had nothing to do with informing." But he told me that he had been disturbed because "the idea of informing" was "turned around" in *On the Waterfront:* "At the time, I felt that it was a terrible misuse of the theme.")

When Kazan and Schulberg had appeared before the Committee, both were resoundingly successful. Therefore, many believed that they had performed as witnesses merely to safeguard their careers in films—which both subsequently denied. (Kazan said that his salary was cut in half after his testimony, and that his former Party membership had damaged his professional life.) However, many felt that if the two had refused to aid the Committee, Kazan could have continued to direct plays on Broadway— since the theater didn't maintain a cast-iron blacklist—and that Schulberg could have gone on writing fiction.

But Kazan plunged to the extreme of publishing a lengthy paid advertisement in *The New York Times,* denouncing the Communists and deploring his year and a half in the Party: "Firsthand experience of dictatorship and thought control left me with an abiding hatred of these. It left me with an abiding hatred of Communist philosophy and methods and the conviction that these must be resisted always." He also wrote that citizens who were "in possession" of the "facts" about Communism "had an obligation to make them known, either to the public or to the appropriate Government agency"—that is, he advised them to follow his example and become informers. He was soon christened "Looselips" by Zero Mostel.

Schulberg offered fifteen names to the Committee, and Kazan volunteered sixteen. While most of them were already familiar to the investigators, each man provided a few that had not been mentioned before. Schulberg spoke about the writers Harry Carlisle and Tillie Lerner, and Kazan referred to Louis Leverett, the co-leader of his Party unit, trade unionist Andrew Overgaard, performer-director Art Smith, and actor Tony Kraber. When Kraber heard Kazan's testimony cited by the Committee, he asked, "Is this the Kazan that signed the contract for five hundred thousand dollars the day after he gave names to this Committee?" An investigator answered, "Would it change the facts if he did?" and Kraber replied, "Would you sell your brothers for five hundred thousand dollars?"

Kazan claimed that his connections with "front organizations were so slight and so transitory that I am forced to rely on a listing of these prepared for me after research by my employer, Twentieth Century-Fox." Fox, like the other studios, had been helped in the "research" by such groups as the American Legion—which furnished producers with dossiers on suspects, as did Hearst columnist George Sokolsky, who was as potent as Roy Brewer in deciding who could (or couldn't) work in Hollywood. Kazan also told the Committee that he had given a copy of his affidavit to Spyros P. Skouras, the president of Fox.

Widely disparaged among their contemporaries, roasted by the Left and some liberals as well as by ex-Communists, never forgiven by some, Kazan and Schulberg have replied to their detractors with considerable heat, enunciating their contempt for the American Communist Party and its tactics. Both have repeated how shocked they were by the Moscow trials and by the suppression of writers in the Soviet Union. Schulberg had also been very upset by the Communists' assault on his first novel, *What Makes Sammy Run?*, which was praised by *The Daily Worker* and then pronounced "reactionary" and "diseased" ten days later—by the same reviewer. In hindsight he compared his problems about the novel to those of Soviet writers who could be sent to the concentration camps, or even executed, for writing books that didn't chime with the Party line. Schulberg told me that after the second review of *What Makes Sammy Run?* John Howard Lawson and other Communists called a meeting at the Hollywood-Roosevelt Hotel and asked him if he wanted to come and defend himself. He reflected that "If I were Russian, I wouldn't be invited to the Hollywood-Roosevelt: I might be on my way to the camps."

Those who criticized Schulberg and Kazan have answered that their positions on the Soviet Union and the Communist Party are perfectly reasonable—but that, in the Fifties, it was indefensible to collaborate with the Committee because any form of cooperation lubricated the machine and enlarged the Committee's success—that giving names condoned and perpetuated the political inquisitions. Hence some non-Communists refused to deny Party membership to the Committee, because answering questions also implied that the Committee had the right to investigate a person's political beliefs. Moreover, the repetition of certain names further blackened the reputations of those who had been (or soon would be) discharged. Some also asked why—if Kazan and Schulberg so sincerely hated Communism—they waited to combat it until it was necessary for them to testify; at that point, they simply had to comply if they wanted any more work in Hollywood.

When I consulted Kazan and Schulberg in the late Seventies, both were generous with their recollections about their movies and their opinions, but neither would discuss his testimony: the subject was surrounded with barbed wire. It was rather as though they had taken the Fifth Amendment. But they did speak freely about *On the Waterfront*. Afterward, I returned to the film: to see how it transcended or reflected its origins, to weigh its relationship to the past.

·

It's my instinct that the enormous emotional impact of *On the Waterfront* won't diminish over the decades, and that the film is a perennial—its aesthetics sustained by Marlon Brando's performance, Leonard Bernstein's racking score, and the dockside crowd scenes where shared hopelessness or determination pass like waves through the clusters of stationary men. Unlike most movies of the

Marlon Brando as a rueful witness in On the Waterfront.

period, which were set in affluent or comfortable surroundings, *On the Waterfront* made the daily experiences and the interior lives of laborers tangible to a middle-class audience. The atmosphere of hard work and poverty, the desperate need for jobs and wages, the sheer difficulties of surviving, are conveyed with a probity that shames a film like *The Grapes of Wrath*—where the poor were merely pathetic, glazed with a facile sentimentality which made their plight seem unreal. Yet *On the Waterfront* also imparts the humor of threadbare people: the jibes and sudden comebacks that can shore up their frayed resilience.

Brando hasn't ever matched his quality in *On the Waterfront*: the utterly urban creature—"I don't like the country, crickets make me nervous"—not overly bright but extremely thoughtful, capable of swift retaliation or the reflex of wryness. Some of his best shrugs occur in this movie, where his shoulders respond to every mood from flirtatiousness to dejection. In the Actors Studio tradition, he's superb at reliving his physical memories, such as an early boxing match, or at fighting for pointless self-control when he's half in tears but not quite weeping over his brother's corpse. (The anguish shared by the siblings after Rod Steiger pulled a gun on Brando, and both were forced to confront the bonds of mutual betrayal, resulted in one of the most passionate scenes between two men that has been filmed.) Brando is also deft at playing dumb when the character wants to be self-protective, and dwelling on the defensive is intrinsic to this figure in jeopardy.

Citing some of Lillian Hellman's personae, such as those in *The Little Foxes*, Kazan has stressed his aversion to "easy villians" and to characters who are labeled as angelic or malign. Instead, ambivalence intrigues him—hence the role reversals between the "good" and "bad" brothers in *East of Eden*. The Brando role in *On the Waterfront* was also contrived as an uneasy villain, a person whom many spectators would repudiate until the script demands that he be respected. Still, if the character is meant to be ambivalent, the plot is not: only one course of action is open to the man who is asked to give names.

The theme of informing that surges through the movie is still very sensitive territory for Schulberg and Kazan. Both insist that the issue of exposing a perfidious trade union sustains the film's narrative on its own—which is true. However, Schulberg argued that only Communists regarded the movie as a plea for the informer—which isn't true—and he declared that *On the Waterfront* was not intended as a justification of the film makers' helpful testimony before the Committee: "I don't think we needed an apology!" Still, he conceded that the experiences overlapped. Kazan concurred, though he did say to me, "Some took it as an apology, in part, for my testimony against Communists, which it, I suppose, to a certain minor degree was." He also felt that the attitudes of the Thirties flavored some of the negative criticism of the movie: "The Left glamorized trade unions, whereas we were the first to say that there was such a thing as a corrupt trade union, and that it could be a force of reaction."

The film is constructed so that it's almost impossible to disagree with it: the audience does want Brando to inform against the mobsters, who have already killed two men who planned to talk at the public hearings of the Waterfront Crime Commission. The movie makes silence seem criminal, and it's reiterated that only insiders can dismantle a vicious organization. Yet a witness may be murdered for obeying his private morality:

"If I spill, my life ain't worth a nickel!"
"And what is your soul worth if you don't?"

On the Waterfront emphasizes the bravery of the informer, "the guts" essential to his actions. The Brando character is wretchedly reluctant to testify: many of the scenes of the movie— almost the bulk of the picture—are devoted to the complexity and the agony of that decision. After he finally agrees to cooperate, the film details his suffering and the punishment visited on the person who names others in a just cause; even decent people despise him: "My friends don't want to talk to me." Though the ending—where the thrashed, bleeding hero with eyeballs rolling upward staggers triumphantly toward his apotheosis—is a festival of bathos, the feelings that lacerate him throughout the movie are absolutely convincing.

And yet the conclusion reverberates with a deceptive optimism; in keeping with the movie's preliminary title, which avers that "self-appointed tyrants can be defeated by right-thinking people in a vital democracy," it appears as though the informer has served to purify the union—even though the nefarious boss promises, "I'll be back." Meanwhile, it's worth pondering the role of the Catholic priest (Karl Malden) who urges Brando to testify—just as the church encouraged the troops of the anti-Communist crusade. Both Malden and Eva Marie Saint function dramatically as Brando's conscience: they make him feel guilty until he does appear before the Crime Commission. These characters are valid for the dockside culture; Kazan said that the heroine was modeled on the young Catholic women whom he'd known in catechism school, and he complimented their "rectitude."

But Malden seems almost superhuman, and he calls the murder of a potential informer "a crucifixion." And Brando's climactic walk reminded a few critics of Christ bearing the weight of the cross. One wonders if Kazan and Schulberg felt that they had been crucified for their testimony, and if—as very bitter ex-Communists—they had lauded the Catholic church in deference to its powers during the political investigations. It's notable that two apparent agnostics chose to steep their movie in glorified Christianity and to use a priest as a moral mouthpiece. (Kazan told me, "Of course I hate religion—I was one of those kids who was *made* to go to catechism school.") As an enemy of puritanism and censorship, Kazan had a lively feud with Cardinal Spellman over *Baby Doll* in 1956, when Spellman ascended the pulpit of Saint Patrick's Cathedral for the first time since 1949, to warn Catholics to stay away from the "evil" and "revolting" picture under "pain of sin," and Kazan declared that he was "outraged" by the charges. Priests were sent to the lobbies of movie theaters, where they wrote down the names of their parishioners who were attending the film.

Although *On the Waterfront* makes a seamless crime story, the political parallels are inescapable—even though the film makers disown them. (I should add that I didn't detect the social metaphor in the Fifties: as an apolitical English major, I was gripped by the film's fervor without realizing its relevance.) When Brando

is accused of being "owned" by the mob's boss, one recalls that the American Communists were said to be "owned" by Moscow. In the movie, the wealthy shipowners who ignore the sovereignty of the criminals are hardly represented, though we do see one from behind while he's watching the hearings on television. Brando's devastating emotional dilemma—when informing means that he will "rat on" his own brother—revives the fact that many felt that the informers of the Cold War had betrayed a brotherhood. A pigeon, a cheese-eater, a canary who sang, stooled, ratted, spilled his guts: the script is rich in the terms that the Left applied to friendly witnesses, although the language is also appropriate to the waterfront. Today, we can't help but regard the movie as an impassioned defense of the informer, and as a petition for sympathy for the pain inflicted by the wrath of his former friends.

When I questioned Schulberg on this matter, he immediately replied that both the Mafia and the Watergate conspirators would have remained inviolable if everyone had remained silent. So I asked if he equated American Communists with criminals. He answered, "I thought they were accessories to murder"—referring to the Thirties and Forties, when they rationalized the guilt of the defendants in the Moscow trials and did not protest the mass liquidations of the Stalin era. He added that he believed that the American Communists would have behaved in the same way if they had won control of this country—"Not that they were going to win." Schulberg also said that they couldn't admit that they "were party to the worst oppression of the twentieth century." He had veered far from the discussion of his screenplay, and he seemed to be stirred by vestigial emotions.

←

Karl Malden as the waterfront priest.

(OVERLEAF) Time *called* Baby Doll *"Just possibly the dirtiest American-made motion picture that has ever been legally exhibited"—although there was little explicit sex in the film, which was one of Kazan's best; it was also Tennessee Williams's finest screenplay. However, due to the stress on thumb-sucking, some assumed that oral sex was implied.*

417-383

Thus, Kazan and Schulberg persisted in deploring the transgressions of the American Communist Party. And yet they continued to define themselves as ultra-liberals, even as radicals, contending that they were still members of "the anti-Stalinist" Left—which was highly unusual for cooperative witnesses. Most who had done penance for their youthful Party membership had then recoiled vehemently from any whisper of liberalism.

Three years after *On the Waterfront*, Kazan and Schulberg made *A Face in the Crowd*, which was intended as a critique of American values—again, that was exceptional for Hollywood in the Fifties. The film, a forceful, imaginative melodrama, explored manipulation and mind control in the context of television. Apart from *Citizen Kane*, few movies had examined monsters of the media; the director and the screenwriter saturated themselves in Madison Avenue and questioned politicians—including Stuart Symington and Lyndon Johnson—about the place of television in politics. The film makers contemplated how much more powerful Huey Long would have been if he'd had television at his disposal, and they remembered the effect of Richard Nixon's Checkers broadcast. Schulberg told me that they also had Joseph McCarthy in mind—as a man who had "used television to destroy others until it helped to destroy him."

Although the central character of *A Face in the Crowd*—a folksy fraud who gathers political momentum until he becomes an adviser to a presidential candidate—may seem like a redneck relative of Schulberg's Sammy Glick, the film makers also employed traits from Will Rogers, Walter Winchell, Arthur Godfrey, and radio's "Uncle Don." Kazan drew a superb performance from Andy Griffith as a monomaniac of volcanic energies who ruins his own career, and Patricia Neal was extremely touching as she became more vulnerable to the ogre for whom she was a midwife. The packaging of politicians was analyzed to a degree that was prophetic, but although the movie received favorable reviews, it didn't attract a wide audience. Some thought its view of television was overstated—as history has proved that it wasn't.

After the riots in Watts in 1965, Schulberg founded the Writ-

Denounced as a stool pigeon, Brando discovers that his own birds have been strangled.

ers Workshop there; in 1970, he and Kazan wanted to make a film about the Young Lords, the radical Puerto Rican group, but they were unable to raise the money. Both men were supportive of those who opposed the war in Vietnam; their loathing of the Communists of the Thirties did not prevent them from endorsing the New Left of the Sixties—which alarmed many of their contemporaries who had come to abhor mass movements.

•

Arthur Miller made no public statement about Kazan's testimony in 1952; in 1956, when the Committee probed Miller about his relationship with Kazan, Miller said that he had "never attacked" the director. Nor did Kazan discuss Miller's position for the record; however, *The New York Times* noted in 1959 that Miller "withdrew his friendship" after Kazan had testified. (Miller—who did not challenge the Committee's right to investigate his politics—had been convicted of contempt of Congress after his hearing; he was fined and received a thirty-day suspended sentence, but he was cleared by the courts in 1958.) Miller wrote *The Crucible*—which excoriated accusers and spurious "confessions" as well as witch burners, and above all, those who "sold" their friends—before Kazan had given names. Miller has sometimes objected that the play has been interpreted as more of a political parable than he intended, and that *The Crucible* is primarily concerned with gullibility and "the paranoid possibilities in the human race," but few who lived through the Fifties can divorce it from the image of the Committee.

Miller's *A View from the Bridge*, which was produced on Broadway in 1955, was thought by some liberals to be an answer to *On the Waterfront*. Set in Red Hook, Miller's play centered on an informer—in this case, a longshoreman who told the immigration authorities that two of his wife's Italian relatives had entered this country illegally. The man is not portrayed as a scoundrel, but his unforgivable act destroys his life. As Miller later remarked, the character was vanquished by "the built-in conscience of the community whose existence he had menaced by betraying it."

But Miller emphasizes that he had heard the story of this man during his days on the waterfront in 1949—hence the play was not a direct reply to Kazan's movie. Still, he told me that "it was a kind of attempt to throw a different light on the whole informing theme . . . I suppose the passions of the moment cast it in that mold." Granting that he had been "very upset" by the rash of informing, he stressed that the actions of the Committee—and the fact that it was allowed to exercise such power—outraged him far more than the behavior of the friendly witnesses, and that "the real issue" was the injury done to democracy: "I have never ceased to blame the Committee first and foremost . . . I never felt a *fraction* of my antagonism for the Committee toward any person who [appeared] in front of it." And he added that sympathy should not be withheld from the informers.

In Miller's play *After the Fall*, produced in 1964, there was an ex-Communist who named others; the character says that he has despised the Party for years, and that "I think we *were* swindled; they took our lust for the right and used it for Russian purposes. And I don't think we can go on turning our back on the truth simply because reactionaries are saying it." The close friend whom he names cries, "It astounds me that you can speak of truth and justice in relation to that gang of cheap publicity hounds . . . ! You are terrified! They have bought your soul!" and charges the witness with knuckling under for money; the latter retorts that the other had lied concerning what he knew about the Soviet Union. The informer is called "a moral idiot" and the man whom he identified commits suicide. Many were sure that the informer was based on Kazan, and Kazan himself directed the play. He and Miller had not worked together for over a decade, and some with long memories were stunned—even angered—by the professional association.

(OVERLEAF) *Andy Griffith as the spell-casting charlatan in* A Face in the Crowd. *When François Truffaut reviewed the movie in* Cahiers du Cinéma, *he wrote, "In America, politics always overlaps [with] show business, as show business overlaps [with] advertising."*

•

A cooperative witness—Lee J. Cobb—appeared in *On the Waterfront*. Kazan also hired a graylisted actor—Albert Dekker, who had a small role in *East of Eden*—when the blacklist was still in force. Years later, the themes of informing and betrayal recurred in Kazan's work. In *The Visitors*, a small, searing film which he directed in 1972 from his son's script, two Vietnam veterans take vengeance on a former friend who gave evidence against them after they raped and murdered a young Vietnamese woman. The informer feels that he should have prevented their act, that turning them in was useless—and he regrets having sent his "buddies" to jail. Anxiety pervades the movie, which skillfully balances a My Lai sensibility against a nostalgia for the normal.

Kazan's novel *The Understudy*, published in 1974, features yet another reluctant informer, whose testimony brings an old friend before the grand jury; the narrator has already poached on the man's professional turf and slept with his wife, and guilt seeps through the book's pages. But the informer's valor is extolled by the police—as in *On the Waterfront*, he's testifying against criminals—and he does everything possible to ease his dying friend's last days: the novelist asks us to admire the character for his own brand of loyalty.

And although Kazan and Schulberg have refused to be remorseful about their hours on the witness stand, Schulberg's endeavors on behalf of black and liberal groups, and Kazan's choice of subject matter, suggest that they have not expunged the memory of their role in the Fifties, nor their sense of rejection by those who despised the Committee and the federal inquisitions.

VI: *Unglaring Exceptions*

While the largest American audiences of 1954 watched James Stewart studying his neighbors in *Rear Window*, or Joan Crawford and Mercedes McCambridge shooting it out in *Johnny Guitar*, or Victor Mature fondling Susan Hayward in *Demetrius and the Gladiators*, while many savored the inspired lunacies of *Beat the Devil*, there was one film that most were protected from seeing. *Salt of the Earth*, made independently by blacklisted writers—directed by Herbert Biberman of the Hollywood Ten, written by Michael Wilson, and produced by Paul Jarrico—was presented by the International Union of Mine, Mill, and Smelter Workers, which had been expelled from the CIO in 1950 on charges of Communist domination. The movie was beleaguered from its inception. Filmed in Silver City, New Mexico, *Salt of the Earth* was based on the 1951–1952 strike by the Mexican-American zinc miners of Mine-Mill, who had demanded equality with their Anglo colleagues, as well as safety regulations on the job.

Since the film was shot before the Korean War was over, some right-wingers deduced that the movie was part of a Stalinist conspiracy to encourage a copper miners' strike that would hinder the production of weapons for the war. There were ample prob-

173

lems in hiring a cast and a crew, because many professionals were reasonably afraid that they would be blacklisted if they worked for those who were said to be Communists. Members of the International Alliance of Theatrical Stage Employees, headed by Roy Brewer, were not allowed to participate. The leading actress, Rosaura Revultas, was harried by immigration officials and deported to Mexico as an "illegal alien" before the filming was finished. Vigilantes disrupted the production, shot at the film makers' cars, and thrashed some of the crew.

Meanwhile, Congressman Donald Jackson of California, a member of the Committee, quoted Hearst columnist Victor Riesel in Congress, warning that Communists were making a picture close to the atomic testing grounds of Los Alamos: the subversives' proximity to secret weapons was deemed ominous. (Jackson, who was determined to quash the movie, which he called "a new weapon for Russia," also noted that the film company had "imported two auto carloads of colored people for the purpose of shooting a scene of mob violence"—it didn't occur to him that the black arrivals were actually film technicians.) Other technicians and laboratories declined to work on the sound and film developing; the Pathé laboratories withdrew from the film processing. Distributors boycotted the movie; even after ten years' litigation, the producers failed in their efforts to enforce antitrust laws against the suppression of their film. Roy Brewer had assured Congressman Jackson that the Hollywood AFL Film Council would do "everything" possible to prevent *Salt of the Earth* from being exhibited, and projectionists and theater owners who were members of Brewer's union would not show it. The American Legion forestalled a number of bookings. Still, the movie had sporadic engagements in ten cities. Those who saw it in Los Angeles were urged to park far from the theater because FBI agents were said to be collecting the license plate numbers from cars in the lot beside the movie house.

During the decades since *Salt of the Earth* was released, some visited it as an archeological artifact, and many were at first struck by its ineptitudes: the militant uplift music, the ponderous narration, the utterly evil bosses and the cruelly cackling sheriff pitted against the inherent goodness of the working people. The film didn't seem radical to spectators of the Sixties and Seventies: for movie-goers accustomed to *If . . .* and *Putney Swope* and *M*A*S*H*, there was nothing unusual about a film that deprecated and challenged the system; many found the movie rather dull, and the fact that the film makers were eventually known to have been Communists held little interest for ensuing generations.

But if one re-enters the mentality of the Fifties and also accepts the movie's flaws, one can be moved by certain passages— and astounded by the level of its feminism. The mainly non-professional cast—mostly Mine-Mill workers from Local 890— adds authenticity to the recurrent struggles of the labor movement. The film's vigor springs from its emphasis on the conflicts and bitter tensions between men and women, among those working on the same side; the women who replace the men as picketers assert that they too must be treated as equals—an almost unimaginable concept for the early Fifties, even among Communists, who often discussed "the woman question" but hardly faced it. Actually, *Salt of the Earth* concentrates even more on sexual oppression than class oppression. And there are many touching moments: the women hastening through hills and fields to join the swelling picket line, or the mutinous neighbors carrying an evicted family's furniture back into their house. There are also amusingly effective scenes when a crowd of angry women in jail shouts from behind the bars at the demoralized sheriff, or when their husbands hang up laundry and grapple with domestic difficulties, discovering what women's work is like—and hating it.

In 1954, it was still suspect to declare that corporations exploited their employees, or that "racial minorities" were underpaid or abused on the job, or that a company could be indifferent to the safety and health of its underlings. Only disloyal citizens would choose to discredit our democracy with such distortions; an indignant article in *Films in Review* claimed that the film's "basic situations" were "untrue in terms of American life" and that the movie would be "unbelievable to all except those, here and abroad, who resent the measure of individual freedom that Americans possess." But even if the film makers had been politically spotless, *Salt of the Earth* would not have been produced by any studio in Hollywood.

And yet a few films did venture beyond the boundaries of prudence. However, such movies were more apt to be made if the theme was contained in a metaphor—if the vehicle was a melodrama or a Western. When Carl Foreman was writing *High Noon* in 1952, he deliberately used Gary Cooper's lone marshal combatting some dangerous outlaws in a small town—where no one wants to support him—as a parable for the Committee's onslaught on Hollywood, and for the timidity of the community there. Foreman thought that the movie would be his last in Hollywood. He was subpoenaed while *High Noon* was in production, and he wasn't sure if his political imagery would be understood. He told me that he had been "morosely pleased" when many wrote to tell him that it was.

After Foreman was blacklisted, *High Noon* was severely criticized in the Soviet Union; *Pravda* lambasted it as "a glorification of the individual." Indeed, Cooper's acute solitude in crisis—as the enemy approaches and even well-meaning people recoil from the inevitable confrontation—gives the film a stark strength which hasn't aged. It was clever to ally the rebellious figure with law and order. Cooper's performance was surely his best, especially because the character was allowed to show quiet twinges of fear: the eyes that widen with shock or pain or disappointment make the stubbornness seem all the more courageous. (The actor was then afflicted with ulcers, which probably enhanced the wincing.) The movie also succeeds due to the sense of urgency: time is horribly short before the town will be destroyed by forces from which it won't recover. As crowds wait at the railway station for the killers' arrival, the film's only possible fallacy is the assumption that a train will run on schedule.

To my knowledge, the one movie that openly protested the tactics of the Committee was *Storm Center*, which was directed and co-written by Daniel Taradash in 1956. The film was conceived and scripted in secrecy because the film makers were certain that it was "politically explosive"; production was postponed several times during five years. Bette Davis plays a mettlesome librarian who refuses to remove a volume called *The Communist Dream* from the shelves after the local city council demands that she do so. She argues that the book is "preposterous"—hence it should be read, like *Mein Kampf.* Accused of turning the library into "a propaganda machine for the Kremlin," she's smeared for her former membership in wartime Communist front groups, and then fired.

The movie is careful to state that Davis is a civil libertarian, not a radical. Branded as "a danger to the community," she finds that adults and children shrink from speaking to her. Another actress might have made the role too pious or pitiful, but Davis's defiant poise protects the film from sogginess. Joe Mantell embodies the sour anti-intellectual of the Fifties: hostile even to his wife's fondness for music and his son's appetite for reading—"I'm stuffed to my gizzard with his library and your piano"—he distills a triumphant loathing of "pinkos." When the library is set on fire by an hysterical child, this modest, simpleminded film does convey the horror of book burning, especially when a large dictionary catches flame—even though the scene was enacted on a movie set, those were real books.

Antipathy toward cultivated persons is also featured in Sidney Lumet's first film, *Twelve Angry Men,* where rude clods like Lee J. Cobb and Ed Begley attack their patrician fellow juror Henry Fonda for his "bleeding heart"—because he's uncertain if an apparent delinquent is definitely guilty of murdering his father. The script by Reginald Rose pitches vulgarians against the genteel and the sensitive: *Twelve Angry Men* was rather disdainful of a mass audience. Yet the movie, which questions our jury system with some gusto, was also quite bold for 1957, when I was startled by

(OVERLEAF) *Gary Cooper fails to enlist the support of his fellow townsmen against a common enemy in Fred Zinnemann's* High Noon.

its outspokenness—mainly because it explored ambiguity and the elusiveness of facts, and because the soft-shelled liberal that Fonda played was almost a magnet for the ridicule of the Right. Today the film seems inhibited; it refers to "personal prejudice" without acknowledging that racism is a part of our society, and the movie begins and ends with a resounding tribute to justice: as the camera soars admiringly up the stout pillars of the New York courthouse to stirring music, the film assures us of fairness and equality under American law. Considering what we've learned since then about the trials of the black and the poor, we can't share the optimism that the film exudes. And yet—naive and old-fashioned as the movie now appears, cramped by its origins as a television play—it did water some seeds which had been parched in Hollywood.

•

The cycle of what were called "Negro problem pictures" that had subsided in 1950 after *No Way Out* had a few descendants in the late Fifties, but the products seem extremely dated. In Martin Ritt's *Edge of the City* (1957), Sidney Poitier is a dockworker who's far too noble to be believable: almost an archangel, he dies protecting his white friend, John Cassavetes. Poitier himself has said that the idealized "other-cheek-turners" that he then played reflected a certain uneasiness on the part of white film makers: a black protagonist had to be so saintly that it would be criminal to mistreat him. Such films continued to indicate that white racists were incredibly wicked or subhuman or mentally ill—they were not normal Americans.

Poitier was allowed a much harsher role in Stanley Kramer's *The Defiant Ones* (1958), which was co-scripted by blacklisted screenwriter Nedrick Young under a pseudonym, but again, the plot obliged Poitier to sacrifice himself out of loyalty to Tony Curtis. The two were cast as escaped convicts chained together: while they stumbled through muddy swamps in flight from the sheriff's dogs, the metaphor was belabored as the two antagonists realized that a black man and a white man could share friendship as well as common oppression. As in *Edge of the City*, Poitier puts the

Storm Center: *Joe Mantell as a truculent middle American who associates education and culture with Communism, and Bette Davis as the librarian whose liberalism becomes the target of local redbaiters.*

white's needs way ahead of his own. And yet, despite the fenced-in roles that he was given until the Sixties, Poitier's talents transcended his image as a superior person whom only miscreats would abuse, and he brought scope and individuality to parts where almost none existed.

•

Films that float outside the mainstream of a period can sometimes reveal the misgivings of that era; if *Storm Center* was a rarity, Samuel Fuller's Korean war movie, *The Steel Helmet* (1951), was a mutant: a blunt picture that's fascinating for its willful contradictions. Fuller's combat films are sometimes hard to follow because he meant them to be: the director was intent on conveying the chaos of war. Fuller dedicated *The Steel Helmet* to the U.S. Infantry, in which he fought during World War II. But his infantrymen are characterized as equally brutal and beefwitted. For them, all Koreans are "gooks"; yet the Americans show lavish contempt for their Korean allies, while praising the intelligence of the enemy. A soldier who admits that "They all look alike to me" is informed, "He's a South Korean when he's running with you, and a North Korean when he's running after you." The script continues to express the Americans' bewilderment about the identity of the enemy, along with their delusion that all Communists must really be Russians; there are references to "rice paddies crawlin' with Commies—just ready to slap you between two pieces of rye bread and wash you down with fish eggs and vodka!" While some of Fuller's movies, such as *China Gate*, are mined with anti-Communism, Fuller's work suggests an anarchist's sensibility that defies any engine of authority—rather than a right-wing point of view.

Filmed in ten days, just after the Korean War began, the movie almost flaunts its low budget: much of the action occurs in a temple where you might expect to be served with fried rice and egg roll—it evokes the fast food school of worship, encircling a buddha that's more Aztec than Oriental. And yet *The Steel Helmet* is sardonically serious—as well as intentionally ugly. Fuller made

Gene Evans defending a Korean temple in The Steel Helmet.

the central sergeant (Gene Evans) so exuberantly sadistic that we can't ever side with him: foul to his men and to all Koreans, he seems to personify the derangement that perpetuates a fruitless war.

The film dwells on American racism, yet the man who voices it most clearly is a venomous North Korean prisoner who taunts a Nisei and a black soldier for defending the country that degrades them: the "liberal" lines are given to the enemy, who calls the black stupid and spits in his face. Meanwhile, the movie makes war seem both idiotic and thoroughly disgusting: while the soldiers fight to save their own lives, nothing justifies their deaths. In 1967, Fuller said that his films were "very anti-war," and he stressed that he exults in contradictions—as well as in characters who can't be classified as good or bad. Hence the ebullient ironies of his mordant, pessimistic action films, such as *Pickup on South Street* (1953), where minor lawbreakers are horrified to be mistaken for Communists, and a surly pickpocket becomes a patriot. Still, *The Steel Helmet*—which earned handsome profits—must have puzzled the audiences of 1951, since most of the Americans are made to seem as repellent as the Communists, and the movie that censures war is also a diatribe against un-Americanism. Columnist Victor Riesel called it a left-wing movie, while *The Daily Worker* pronounced it "so reactionary that it might have been financed by Douglas MacArthur." And the Pentagon was incensed because the film showed an American soldier shooting an unarmed prisoner of war.

In the early Fifties, the studios maintained the wartime tradition of showing scripts to army or navy officials for their approval—in exchange for permission to film troops and military equipment. Since *From Here to Eternity* included an incompetent officer and a bestial sergeant, the screenwriter softened several situations that would have displeased the Pentagon. Soon afterward, the navy objected that *The Caine Mutiny* was anti-American; they protested that the character of Captain Queeg gave them a bad image and that they had never had a mutiny. Producer Stanley Kramer had to convince the Secretary of the Navy and the Chief of Naval Operations that he didn't intend to impair the navy's reputation—in order to be allowed to photograph destroyers and aircraft carriers. Still, as late as 1959, the government refused to lend Kramer a nuclear submarine for *On the Beach*, and he had to defend himself before a congressional committee concerning "world guilt" about nuclear weapons.

And yet, after Korea, a few American movies like *Attack!* did criticize the conduct of the military. In 1957, both *The Bridge on the River Kwai* and *Paths of Glory* deplored the mentalities that are prone to waste the lives of others; the attitude toward leadership had altered hugely since the feverishly patriotic films of World War II. Still, the targets of *The Bridge on the River Kwai* were British officers, while *Paths of Glory* denounced some French generals of 1916; it's very doubtful that such a film could have been made about the American army, when most of the Cold War movies were still very protective of all our institutions. Neither film questions the necessity of war, but both raise savage questions about the nature of heroics.

Carl Foreman purchased the rights to Pierre Boulle's novel, *The Bridge on the River Kwai*; he wrote the screenplay anonymously while he was on the blacklist. At Foreman's suggestion, Michael Wilson (who was also blacklisted) joined him for the final scene-polishing. Boulle received an Oscar for the script, although the French novelist couldn't write in English at that time. But many knew that Foreman and Wilson had written the movie, even though director David Lean didn't give them any credit for it.

The British film industry embraced *The Bridge on the River Kwai* as an English film, due to Lean and because it starred Alec Guinness and Jack Hawkins, while the Americans claimed it as their own, since they financed and produced it and contributed William Holden. Despite the Hollywood sheen, the movie is far more complex than most American pictures of the Fifties. As Guinness's troops of British prisoners diligently build the bridge that will abet the enemy, while Hawkins's team conspires to destroy it, the emphasis on obsession—which means dying for "a matter of principle"—is tautened by the realization that the chances for survival are almost nil.

Guinness's rigid colonel isn't a simple fanatic: although he's blind to his collaboration with the Japanese, he has a misguided integrity that we're forced to esteem—just as we're made to sympathize with the Japanese commanding officer (Sessue Hayakawa), whom Guinness treats as an inferior, almost like a servant. Jack Hawkins's humorous, offhand autocracy keeps the Guinness role from being a caricature of British cool. Yet all that Anglo-Saxon phlegm would be insufferable if it weren't balanced by a trashy American upstart's outrage at the old-school valiance: William Holden berates the English for being "crazy with courage," for planning to die like gentlemen instead of living like human beings.

Apart from the muddled climax, and the unnecessary cries of "Madness! Madness!" the film's moral dilemmas are as binding as ever. The blistered faces and ruined shoes of the prisoners who march in place to "Colonel Bogey" are still moving: that mass of whistling men conveys the vulnerability of any group to authority gone awry, or authority in the wrong hands—the officials or politicians whose megalomania can make rubble of us all.

The British officers in *The Bridge on the River Kwai* are at least semi-human, but the French generals in Stanley Kubrick's *Paths of Glory* are monstrous. As they send eight thousand war-torn men on a mission that's known to be impossible, this amazingly bitter film makes one truly hate the military—as *The Bridge on the River Kwai* does not, since it blames only individuals and their training. The elegant French generals regard the working-class soldiers as objects, or as animals of no value. But the mass slaughter ordered for the sake of the generals' prestige inspires an observer to quote Samuel Johnson on patriotism: "The last refuge of a scoundrel."

Filmed from above, the doomed men crawling across the

$\rightarrow$

Alec Guinness in The Bridge on the River Kwai; *the movie respects but also challenges the work ethic: Guinness's bridge belongs to the death railway that could help to defeat the Allies.*

earth look particularly helpless, while the light from rockets exploding over their heads exposes the corpses that many will become—while others struggle clumsily out of the trenches, yelling to give themselves courage. Thousands are killed or wounded before they can walk three steps. The repetitive drum rolls on the soundtrack emphasize the futility of the maneuver: as stumbling figures fall and fail to rise, the film ravages our emotions with the anonymity of the almost or already dead.

The generals define the survivors as "scum" who are guilty of "insubordination." The film then shifts from simultaneous suffering to the agonies of three soldiers whom the generals choose to execute for cowardice, as an example to the others: this trinity must pay for the generals' mistakes. One of the condemned men had won many citations for bravery: now, as he's dying of a fractured skull, his cheek is pinched so that he will open his eyes before he's shot. The film muses on the fragile distinctions between living and dying: during his final supper, another prisoner reflects that a cockroach in his cell will outlive him, and later he laughs and weeps at the realization that he hasn't "had a sexual thought" since the court-martial began.

As the bodies slump before the firing squad, the movie permits no hope of justice, and the rest of the mangled troops are immediately sent back to the front. It seems astonishing that this film was made in the complacent, timorous Fifties—and it nearly wasn't: the major studios rejected the project until Kubrick enlisted Kirk Douglas as the star. Even so, the movie was released with a disclaimer that the conduct of these troops didn't represent the millions of other French soldiers who fought so splendidly throughout World War I.

Aside from *The Bridge on the River Kwai* and *Paths of Glory*, few war films were produced after the early Fifties; by then, it was difficult to revive the enemies of World War II: the swinish or cruelly refined Nazis had been overworked by Hollywood, and so had the vermin known as the Japanese. New adversaries were needed, and already they had come from outer space—armed with deadlier weapons and viler conspiracies than our planet had ever known.

✱ I was astonished when I saw it at Gunter Air Force Base in 1957: what a war movie!

Paths of Glory: *Adolphe Menjou as one of the corrupt generals, with
Richard Anderson as a major. The script, written by Stanley Kubrick,
Calder Willingham, and Jim Thompson, stresses that guiltless soldiers are
being "murdered" to protect the generals' reputations. The film was
banned for some years in France.*

VII: *Watch the Skies*

At a time when numerous Americans were afraid of one another—when the Right feared the Left, when the Left feared the Right, when many moderates feared contamination from either side—even our broadest forms of entertainment mirrored the national malaise. The science fiction movies of the Fifties have often been called paranoid: the scenarios were dominated by hostile forces that were eager to enslave or obliterate us. The imagery and the language did reflect the atmosphere of the Cold War and the Korean War, and these movies reinforce the conviction that we must defend ourselves against invaders—an obsession that may have been all the more acute because we had never experienced a war on our own turf.

Hollywood had made very few science fiction films before 1950. Those that were produced in the Thirties—mostly by the British—tended to be futuristic fantasies, evoking the world several thousand years from now. There, people in togas clambered in and out of quaint machines, or strolled through plazas while uttering lines like, "Our Brother, the Giver of Power, is yonder." Graham Greene complained in his movie reviews that the citizens of the future also wore Tudor costumes—in short, they seemed to belong to the past.

191

Throughout World War II, there was almost no filmed science fiction: the genre had minimal appeal during global war. A few of the early postwar space movies suggested a return to the frontier and a revival of the pioneer spirit among those who set off to explore the moon. Subsequently, the extremely pessimistic pictures of the Fifties were constructed to be frightening (in contrast to some of the cheerful, humorous, and quasi-religious science fiction movies of recent years, such as *Close Encounters of the Third Kind*). The Fifties films pilfered the plots of turn-of-the-century novels of H. G. Wells and Jules Verne, who had had faith in science and in progressive possibilities for the future—a viewpoint that was moribund in the cinematic visions of the Fifties. However, despite Wells's commitment to science, he was skeptical about our ability to cope with an intergalactic crisis, as was evident from *The War of the Worlds*; the tone of that novella, which emphasizes our helplessness in the face of the Martians' assault, was reproduced in Hollywood's science fiction.

Earnestness was a key ingredient of these movies: throughout *Them!*—in which giant ants run amok—no one ever smiles, and there's not a single kiss in the movie. Bemusement or incomprehension are necessary to the expository scenes, where people keep saying, "Wait a minute, this just doesn't make *sense!*" or "Do you think I'm crazy? I saw those things with *my own* two *eyes!*" or "I know it sounds *insane*, but—" and the actors' eyes must widen while their jaws drop. (Because of all the protestations, I'm unable to read much science fiction, but that very bewilderment is what I relish on the screen.) There have to be lulls between astonishments—complete with mundane remarks, such as "Why don't you get something to eat?"—and understatement adds a certain spice: in the midst of a diversionary sandstorm, someone is apt to say soberly, "Quite a breeze," or, when beset by vibrations from Jupiter, "Very strange. Most unusual." False reassurance is really a brand of prophecy: "I guess there's nothing here that won't wait until morning" means that pandemonium is imminent. Above all, disbelief is essential to science fiction: those who disregard or deride reports of astral ghouls or crab monsters impatiently tell the frantic witness to be realistic, or that he's been dreaming, or to harness his imagination; the latter's panic increases as he's chided for circulating "idiotic stories."

A number of the movies dwelled on the aftereffects of the atom bomb, when lingering radiation from atomic testing caused creatures to grow to demonic proportions or reactivated dead dinosaurs and brought prehistoric ogres back to life. Occasionally, radioactivity reduces normal size: the hero of *The Incredible Shrinking Man* becomes a pathetic homunculus, terrorized by his pet cat or a spider. In *Them!* (directed by Gordon Douglas, who also directed *I Was a Communist for the FBI*), homicidal ants larger than mastodons appear in the desert, just where the bomb was first tested in 1945. Guilt shimmers through the film, which—like many others—somberly states that the disaster is the fault of mankind, since our science was responsible for the ghastly mutations. A doctor deduces that "We may be witnesses to a biblical prophecy come true" when "the beasts shall inherit the earth," and he was correct: the American screen was then deluged with colossal wasps, grasshoppers, tarantulas, and locusts in a slew of insect movies.

It's repeated that the ingenious ants, like most Martians, have an appalling talent for "social organization," which sounds like a Bolshevik trait. Unless all the ants are killed, the human race will be extinct—within a year. Therefore, although we're to blame for the deadly phenomena, the punishment outstrips our errors. But our supernatural enemies are always endowed with an intelligence that's far superior to ours; characteristic of the Fifties, intellect was suspect—in these movies, it was often evil. Martian technology outdistanced our latest inventions, as we feared that the Russians' might, especially after their first atomic explosion in 1949, and again when they launched the Sputnik in 1957. Moreover, the Martians had monitored our broadcasts for years—hence they could speak English, when we didn't know their language—and

(OVERLEAF) *Ants on the rampage in* Them! (1954).

they knew how to fly to our planet when we had no idea how to visit theirs. Meanwhile, they constantly studied us and spied on us—while we remained ignorant of their very existence.

Apprehension permeates the films, and some of the aliens are as fearful of us as we are of them. In *It Came from Outer Space* (1953), the rather decent Martians can't trust humans because we "destroy what we don't understand." Considering the right-wing perspective of most science fiction movies, Robert Wise's *The Day the Earth Stood Still* (1951) is a surprisingly liberal film: there, a saintly interplanetary visitor (Michael Rennie) arrives on a peace mission to warn that our international animosities are imperiling the entire universe, and that our weapons will blow up all the planets if world leaders don't settle their differences—again, there's a stress on the violent nature of our society. (On Rennie's planet there are no wars, and atomic energy is used for peaceful purposes.) The movie also asks how we would behave if Christ returned to earth: the answer is that we would shoot him. In conclusion, the script insists once more that we must mind our nuclear manners—an exceptional theme for a picture of the Fifties. Otherwise, when space folk alighted among us, they were determined to annihilate our civilization—or to capture our best brains and compel them to solve their own problems.

The heroes—really saviors—of the films are rugged military men or FBI agents; tanks and troops and flamethrowers defend the petrified population from mutants or an avalanche of ectoplasm. The officers and investigators disdain book learning and scientists, and they're always inclined to demolish the mysterious, even when the object is amicable. (In those days, almost no one was going to contradict the Pentagon or to accuse the FBI of malpractice.) Inevitably, the authorities declare that the national emergency must be kept secret for as long as possible: there's no confidence at all in the public, which will go berserk if frightened—as some Americans did during the legendary Orson Welles broadcast of *The War of the Worlds* in 1938. Thus, fear is dangerous in itself—even if the fear is rational—and "an epidemic of mass hysteria" is often pivotal to the plots of these movies. But the fixation on secrecy

a holdover from WW2 where civilian panic + "anarchy" were expected to follow air-raids and didn't. (One reason, incidentally, why nuclear weapons became popular

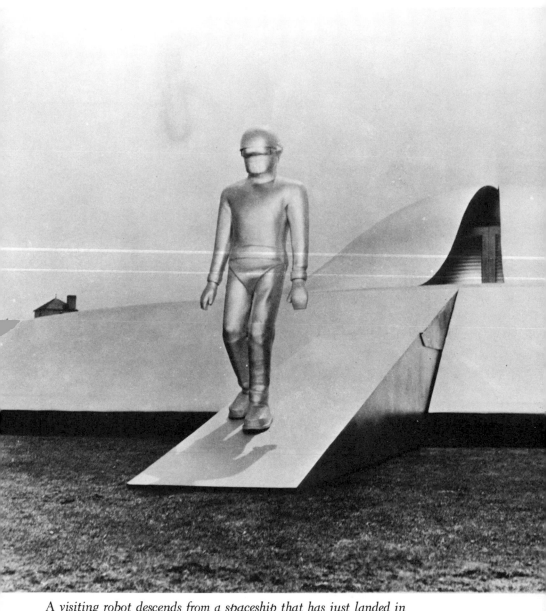

A visiting robot descends from a spaceship that has just landed in Washington in The Day the Earth Stood Still.

with The military – The old "break civilian morale" was replaced by "kill all The civilians" in strategy.

never wavers: people even whisper when they approach extraterres-trials, and it's thought that the creatures can read minds.

Among the items that landed here was *The Blob* (1958), a species of ooze that was the by-product of a fallen meteor, which engorged unwary persons; its dimensions and its power increased with the number of its victims. Leaking under doorsills and through ventilators, it was capable of enveloping the entire conti-nent. (As usual, mortals felt impotent as they shouted to one an-other, "Why don't you do something? Do something!") There was no moral struggle in being absorbed by the Blob, but Steve McQueen waxed desperate in his crusade to persuade his fellow townsmen that creeping slime was actually on the loose. In Chris-tian Nyby's *The Thing* (1951), a huge carnivorous carrot—played by James Arness in what appears to be a baseball cap—crashes at the North Pole in a flying saucer. Able to reproduce itself with fiendish rapidity, it lives on blood and is much wiser than we are; also, it isn't "impeded by emotional or sexual instincts," as it slaughters dogs and men.

Scientists are often obstructionists or troublesome idealists, hence they are the adversaries of the military. In the name of scholarship, the learned men endanger everyone—because they want to preserve the lethal ants' nest or the Thing in the interests of scientific research. A professor like Edmund Gwenn in *Them!* is also tainted by his vocabulary: he uses verbs like "fortify," to which a virile officer retorts, "Why can't we all *speak English?*" The abnormality of intellectuals was featured throughout these movies. And the scientist in *The Thing* (Robert Cornthwaite) is almost as villainous as the super-carrot: in his beard and fur hat, he looks downright Russian and also rather like the Devil as he schemes to protect the creature from the military's efforts to elec-trocute it. Rather plaintively, he says that we can learn so much from the Thing: "All I want is a chance to communicate with it." Finally, he cried to it, "Listen, I'm your friend!" but it smashes him to the floor: friendship means nothing to it. Most of the films end with grim predictions that our cosmic enemies may return to conquer us, and the *The Thing* concludes with the most impassioned plea for vigilance of all: "Tell the world . . . Watch the skies—everywhere—watch the skies!"

The child's role in science fiction is to alert others to the perils that prowl among us. However, as in the family melodramas of the period, children have great difficulty in being heard or understood by their parents: most adults refuse to realize that a crisis exists, and disbelief is rampant when the voice of reason is that of a child. In that respect, William Cameron Menzies' *Invaders from Mars* (1953) has a nightmarish quality: a small boy—who knows that the Martians are kidnapping distinguished citizens and implanting crystals in their brains which will drive them to horrendous deeds—cannot convince his seniors of the facts. Furthermore, his own parents become brutal and sinister figures after their minds are damaged by the Martians' surgery. Traumatized by the duplicity that surrounds him, the boy rushes to the police station, only to discover that the police chief himself is a pawn of the invaders.

The scene is shot from the child's point of view: the camera tilts upward to make the adults look enormous and threatening, and the movie raises the question that recurs throughout science fiction: who can be trusted? Parents who mustn't be trusted and should be feared are even more horrifying to the boy than the Martians—who are seen in repeated footage trotting stiff-kneed through their subterranean tunnels, lumbering from side to side in space suits with long zippers running up their backs. People keep disappearing into quicksand where the Martians lurk underground in a buried spaceship: they take control of individual earthlings and make them commit treasonous acts, while a disembodied silver head enclosed in a plastic ball gives orders like a commissar—the Martians are "slaves to his will." All in all, the parallel between Martians and Communists is quite pronounced in this movie, where those who are programmed to be traitors to America are intent on perverting or suppressing the truth.

The preoccupation with infiltration and mind control was further extended in Don Siegel's *Invasion of the Body Snatchers* (1956). As a result of atomic mutation, plants from another world

GREAT CLOTHES!

Formerly affectionate parents (Hillary Brooke and Leif Erickson)—whose minds have been subverted by the Martians—become a menace to their own child in Invaders from Mars.

gain possession of human bodies, which become "hosts to an alien form of life." As our society is converted into a regime of totalitarian vegetables, the survivors exclaim, "They're taking us over, *cell by cell*," and "It's a malignant disease spreading through the whole country!" In that era, Communism was often compared to fatal *leprosy* illness: in 1952, Adlai Stevenson said in a campaign speech that *in Big* Communism was "a disease which may have killed more people *Jim* in this world than cancer, tuberculosis, and heart disease com- *McClain* bined." Stevenson also said that the goal of America's enemies was "total conquest, not merely of the earth, but of the human mind."

In a film like *Invasion of the Body Snatchers*, when a close friend or relative behaves "unlike himself," the image of brainwashing arises—as it did in the consciousness of the Fifties, when many believed that the American prisoners in Korea had been subjected to thought control. (Because none of the seven thousand prisoners had escaped from captivity, and few had attempted to do so, and since subsequent Senate investigations suggested that about seventy percent of them had collaborated with the Koreans to some extent, it was tempting to think that they had been brainwashed.) In the movie, love is abolished, along with all family ties, and the victims are assured that they will be "reborn into an untroubled world"—which has echoes of a baleful utopianism. Humanoids can look just like the rest of us, as Communists do; but they are not in charge of their own souls, and as their numbers multiply, everyone will become alike. (In the Fifties, many believed that Communist governments turned their citizens into robots.) So the political forebodings of the period spilled over into science fiction, where subservience to alien powers and the loss of free will were so often depicted, and the terror of being changed into "something evil" became a ruling passion. The amusing 1978 remake of *Invasion of the Body Snatchers* did not perpetuate the social overtones—instead, it concentrated on conformity and surrendering the capacity to feel, and few of the scenes had the impact of Kevin McCarthy's climax in the original, when he stood on a highway, screaming at passing trucks and cars, "You fools, you're in danger . . . ! They're after us! You're next! You're next!"

* "communiss" + "Russia" became the philosopher's wall on which we projected our own society —

In the fantasies of the Fifties, God sometimes spoke on the radio when humanity needed correction, as in William Wellman's *The Next Voice You Hear . . .* (1950), where a splenetic middle-class family in a suburb of Los Angeles is magically sweetened after tuning in on God's instructions to count their blessings. These malcontents had erred in thinking that life was frustrating and boring, but God taught them to appreciate middle America, and to accept the status quo. The Deity employs the radio to tackle a more formidable source of sin in Harry Horner's *Red Planet Mars* (1952)—namely, international Communism. The movie, set in the near future, plays on the familiar dread of a nuclear holocaust and the likelihood that we're heading for oblivion. But God takes to the airwaves, and soon Russian peasants are listening raptly to His bulletins on the Voice of America. After hearing a condensed version of the Sermon on the Mount, the peasants pull the pictures of Stalin from their walls and organize an uprising: Russian Christians overthrow the Kremlin and establish a new government, which re-opens all the churches, and the free world pays ecstatic tribute to "a nation finding its soul." The scientists in this movie function as God's servants by decoding His messages, but they perish in an explosion; despite the heavenly defeat of Communism, the sacrificial aspects of this film make it difficult to rejoice in God's manipulation of technology.

Among the ultraviolet rays and the metallic beeps from laboratory equipment, I have an affection for the passages of scientific explanation—as when the scientists haul out charts and dispense such information as "Water reflects light." These scenes are more successful than those in which monstrosities materialize. Since most of the films had meager budgets, many of the special effects or illusions were feeble: the ants in *Them!* resembled clumsy puppets which looked as though a sneeze might dispatch them, the Blob appeared to be a harmless mound of red Jell-O, and when

→

Kevin McCarthy is horrified by the triumph of alien powers in Invasion of the Body Snatchers.

The Creature from the Black Lagoon bellowed, he sounded like an an old Model T Ford. Inspired effects were achieved by Ray Harryhausen, who had a habit of destroying national monuments: in *It Came from Beneath the Sea*, he decimated the Golden Gate Bridge in San Francisco, and elsewhere his flying saucers smashed the Washington Monument and the Capitol. But these procedures were highly expensive, and most science fiction movies were committed to thrift. Therefore, the directors prudently refrained from exhibiting the supernatural too often—instead, the image was allowed to build up in the audience's mind. Meanwhile, the soundtrack could stimulate the spectators' imaginations: the theremin—an early electronic instrument which warbles like a mechanical contralto—was often heard in science fiction. Previously, the theremin was used in *The Lost Weekend* to accompany Ray Milland's delirium tremens, and in *Spellbound* for the psychoses of Gregory Peck; in the Fifties, it was mated to outer space, especially when an unidentified flying object descended on us.

In short, most of the science fiction movies were visually unfrightening. However, the doom-laced scripts yielded metaphors for the larger malignancies of the Cold War, when a neighbor or one's former teacher might suddenly be labeled as a subversive, when a nuclear attack (or accident) might expunge all questions of who was right or who was wrong, or safe or sorry or secure. The future—once an exhilarating concept—grew more ominous: there was no longer any assurance that one had any place in it, that continuity could be counted on.

•

Propelled by the fear of godless Communism, coupled with the impulse to equate faith with success, rooted in the traditional American belief that national or individual prosperity was a sign of God's approval, the religious revival of the early Fifties escalated Bible sales, while Bishop Fulton J. Sheen and the Reverend Billy Graham and the Reverend Norman Vincent Peale basked on the best seller list. While Cardinal Cushing welcomed Joseph McCarthy to prayer breakfasts, politicians hastened to polish the cre-

Scientists were always the acme of gravity in science fiction movies:
Invaders from Mars.

dentials of Christianity, and the Republican National Committee identified Dwight D. Eisenhower as "the spiritual leader of our times"—even though he had rarely attended church in forty years, a practice that he adopted when he became a presidential candidate.

Bishop Sheen's television series, *Life Is Worth Living*, reached twenty million viewers after it commenced in 1952; his political as well as his moral views were heard on one hundred and twenty-three radio stations. In the Thirties, he had supported Franco in the Spanish Civil War, reasoning that "We cannot breed rats in abundance without being obliged to use rat poison, and so neither can we breed Communists without being obliged to use the poison of fascism." In the Fifties he denounced the "colossal wastage of taxes to pay professors who would destroy America by teaching Russian Bolshevism," and he was prominent in converting ex-Communist informers to Catholicism. In the meantime, for middle America, patriotism allied itself with the church, while confidence (in the God-given right of Americans to enjoy what they spent or consumed) and anxiety (about nuclear warfare, a landscape riddled with Communist spies) swept many citizens into the churches, whose attendance had dwindled right after the war was won. As multitudes ingested piety like a tranquilizer, contributions to religious organizations swelled.

Christianity as a commodity—as a wellspring of happiness, as a bulwark against the Red tide—was a boon for Hollywood: Bible epics provided an opportunity to inject action movies with the new religiosity, and to legitimize sexuality on the screen. Even before World War I, titillating scenes had been permissible on the stage as long as they occurred in biblical pageants; later, Cecil B. De Mille had exploited the same formula for silent movies. It was easier to lower a woman's neckline, slit her skirts, or accentuate her breasts in an evangelical context than any other, and sinners could cavort at length when Jehovah was sure to punish them. In fact, biblical movies simply had to illustrate lasciviousness—so that it could be condemned. Some of the actors who played pagans were obviously cast for their pectorals, and there was often a multiplicity of male nipples, which were even more conspicuous than the women's cleavage; many clinches were exchanged by the semi-nude. And when it was said that heathens ate "the bread of wickedness" and that they were "filled" with "vile affections," overhead shots of writhing bodies could evoke an orgy with more cunning than a close-up.

At the heart of the Cold War, some producers were quite willing to indicate a kinship between Roman and Egyptian despots and the Kremlin. De Mille, who felt that there was "a Red band encircling the earth," and that criticism of his *Samson and Delilah* sprang exclusively from Communist sources, accused most of those who disagreed with him of being political deviants; in 1950, he led a campaign to require all members of the Screen Directors Guild to sign a loyalty oath, and he threatened to quote the remarks of his opponents to Joseph McCarthy. He also proposed that directors should file reports with the Guild concerning the politics of everyone who had worked on their last films—so that their colleagues could consult a "loyalty index" when actors or writers applied for jobs. And De Mille's own foundation supplied "information" about suspected left-wingers to the Committee.

De Mille threaded his politics through his second production of *The Ten Commandments* (1956); in a prologue to the movie, he steps in front of a gold curtain to explain that "the theme of this picture is whether men are to be ruled by God's law—or whether they are to be ruled by the whims of a dictator. . . . Are men the property of the state? Or are they free souls under God? This same battle continues throughout the world today." When a slave in the film asks, "Is life in bondage better than death?" we catch a reverberation of "Better dead than Red." The opening narration of Mervyn LeRoy's *Quo Vadis* (1951) stresses that in Imperial Rome, "the individual is at the mercy of the state," and Christ is called "a rebel against the state." The massive audiences that flocked to the Bible movies could not have missed the point.

(OVERLEAF) *Hedy Lamarr in De Mille's* Samson and Delilah (1949). *De Mille defined his movie as "a story of the power of prayer."*

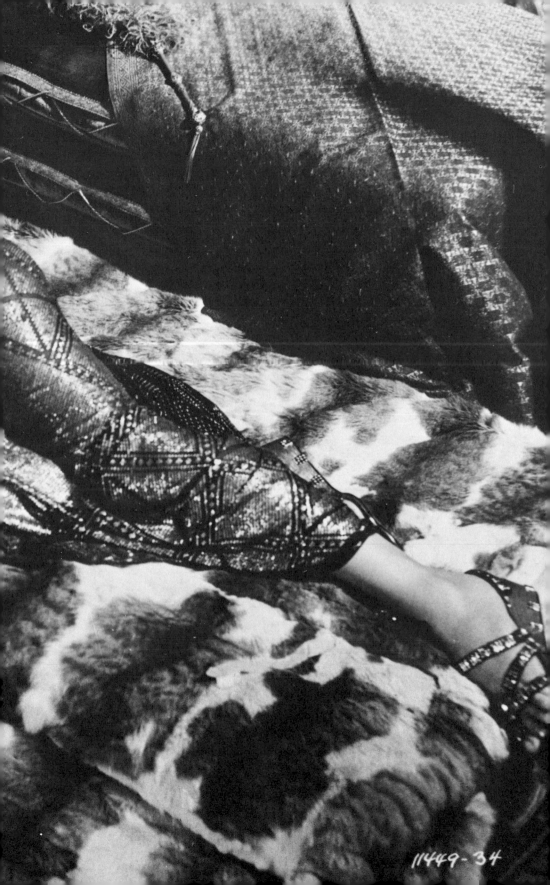

11449-34

Although the Roman palaces or arenas and the Egyptian temples were advertised as the products of scrupulous research, the language and appearance of the biblical personae were aggressively contemporary—presumably in an effort to make theology seem accessible: to reassure the public that religion could be entertaining, that history need not be scholarly or daunting. Sometimes the Romans or Hebrews speak like popular songs: "Love such as mine can never die" and "The night's still young." In *Quo Vadis*, the courtiers keep urging one another to *"Relax,"* and Robert Taylor tells Deborah Kerr that the Christian philosophers "shouldn't be stuffing your luscious little head with such nonsense." In *The Ten Commandments,* Anne Baxter strikes pin-up poses before her mirror and teases Charlton Heston when "the wine of desire is in her veins": "Oh Moses, Moses, you stubborn, splendid, adorable fool." (De Mille wrote in his memoirs that when he addressed writers and actors, he had "to translate the Bible's glorious and hallowed English into the crudest vernacular. It shocks but it makes real.") The revealing costumes of Egyptian royalty resemble twentieth-century loungewear, replete with leopardskin, and almost everyone clanks and jingles: the metal jewelry in the women's hair and around manly necks and the slaves' chains tinkle relentlessly with each dramatic gesture. From frame to frame the movies are as easy to follow as comic books: their infantile nature is highlighted by the fact that the wardrobes and faces and insights—"After all, dying is a part of living"—aren't unfamiliar.

Graham Greene was once asked to revise part of a script for a remake of *Ben-Hur:* producer Sam Zimbalist told him, "You see, we find a sort of anti-climax after the Crucifixion." But there are few such letdowns in the Bible spectaculars of the Fifties, where the action rarely sags: infinite chases—often in chariots, sometimes in catacombs—and duels on staircases over water, toppling temples, feasts, luxuriant battles, and athletic murders main-

→

Victor Mature at the foot of the cross in The Robe: *the actor described this expression as "making with the holy look."*

The man is a genius!

tained their status as adventure films. Christians are given to continuous calisthenics: devotion makes acrobats of them all. The crowds of Hebrews massing for the Exodus in *The Ten Commandments* are reminiscent of a vast roundup in a Western; (in the 1923 version, the Egyptian soldiers were California cowboys, and several hundred orthodox Jews were hired "because," De Mille felt, "they would give the best possible performance as the Children of Israel"). De Mille was extraordinarily gifted at directing legions of extras, and when he sent them marching and singing through the divided waters of the Red Sea, even an atheist was likely to be impressed. Of course the Bible pictures needed mobs and stampedes and exotic vistas in order to fill up the wide screen in Hollywood's attempt to compete with television; the studios hoped that giantism would win back their waning audiences. But although the epics had a titanic success, CinemaScope—which was advertised as "a modern miracle"—and VistaVision and Super-Scope couldn't dent the public's enthusiasm for the small screen.

At the beginning of each film, we know that the most attractive persons will become Christians: faces like Richard Burton's or Deborah Kerr's or Jean Simmons's were selected to see the light, and no incipient Christian could be unalluring. (Bigness demanded even more facial perfection for close-ups than the normal screen did: when the lips are twelve feet across, the gargantuan visages that weep or grin or glower can afford few blemishes.) Transcendent smiles overwhelm all the handsome features, although no one glows quite so forcibly as Victor Mature, who is illumined like a giant jack-o'-lantern. All the epics confirm that Christianity makes people very happy; they feel wonderful as soon as they've embraced the faith. Clouds—as a backdrop for joyful believers—are copious in these films. While the Bible movies acknowledge that Christians suffered for their sanctity—indeed, their tribulations justified lavish scenes of violence, complete with burn-

←

Yul Brynner confronting a miraculous hailstorm in The Ten Commandments.

ing cities, ravening lions, and satanic tortures—they're usually rewarded long before the last reels drench them with delight.

Miracles did not abound in the biblicals until the Sixties, when marvels were plentiful in such movies as Nicholas Ray's *King of Kings* and George Stevens's *The Greatest Story Ever Told*. Some film makers found cinematic miracles distasteful: they thought that movies should not play on superstition. In the New Testament films, Christ is hardly ever shown, and never in a frontal shot: when he makes an occasional guest appearance, we see only his hands or his back. But despite the inhibitions of other producers, De Mille didn't shrink from miracle-making: in *The Ten Commandments*, the Nile runs red, staffs turn into cobras, blood trickles from pagan statues, hail falls from a clear sky, plagues proliferate, flaming comets drill God's laws into the rocks of Mount Sinai, and the burning bush is a microwave extravaganza. Since most of these wonders are menacing or punitive, one's reminded of the science fiction movies: the same apparatus of special effects is used to uplift or alarm. In the realm of the supernatural, the repressed hopes that Christianity can tap were answered by devices that awakened the hidden fears stimulated by the onslaught of extraterrestrials.

Although a few movie miracles are benign—as when Ben-Hur's relatives are cured of leprosy—most are intended to intimidate the witnesses. But the unearthly visitations could hardly have unnerved the audience: the voice of De Mille's God sounds like a warped record when He orders Moses to "Put off thy shoes from off thy feet" in the accents of New York; in the ensuing dialogue it's clear that the Deity has laryngitis. Moreover, He must be a hairstylist, since Moses returns from the mountain with a totally new coiffure—his wife gasps, "Moses . . . your hair"—and it's difficult to venerate a great big wigmaker up in the sky. Therefore, although these movies predated the widespread rumor that God was dead, they rather innocently suggested that He was stale—a certain mustiness pervaded His domain, in spite of all the beards and frescos and armor and torchlit parades that Hollywood assembled to magnify His glory.

CODA

Sifting our cultural sands for change, one finds that movies are slow to receive the imprint. The Vietnam war wasn't fought on film until three years after it had ended, and most actresses' roles showed scant variety until the women's movement had existed for a decade. Yet when Hollywood hastens to be contemporary, the results can be disastrous, as when the studios tried to produce "Now-movies" about "campus disorders" in the late Sixties: the limp yet hectic melodramas that ensued seemed like botched parodies—of film production as well as of the opposition to war and racism.

Because Hollywood is governed by its own interior cycles, setbacks are always temporary; although the Bible pictures had a retrogressive effect on the industry—since filling the large screen with protracted strife or lengthy banquets seemed to dictate that our movies had to be sluggish—the trend was as transient as any. Despite Hollywood's eagerness to borrow the epithet of the New Frontier, the films of the early Sixties contained few innovations until Stanley Kubrick's *Lolita* opened in 1962.

Already an admirer of Kubrick's *Paths of Glory*, I went to his *Spartacus* during a ferocious New York heat wave in search of air conditioning; having chosen the longest movie in town, I was then

215

startled to find that an epic could be so enlivening, unglazed by piety or prurience. But since Kubrick had been hired to direct *Spartacus* at the last moment, he was not in complete control of the movie, nor was he allowed to rework the script by Dalton Trumbo (who was surfacing from the blacklist), and his talents were hampered by the movie's conventions. But the stygian humor of *Lolita* was new to American films: during the Forties and Fifties movie-goers were rarely invited to be amused by desperate characters or situations, and black comedy—which would become a leading genre of the Sixties—had been mainly confined to print until Kubrick brought it to the screen. The extended metaphor of aging, cultivated Europe being manipulated and deceived by ruthless, disarming young America succeeds throughout the film: James Mason's impeccable performance as Vladimir Nabokov's Humbert Humbert conveys the damaged dignity of the autumnal man obsessed with an irritable child, without ever verging on pathos.

Although the Production Code was beginning to ease in 1962, the movie is deliberately unerotic—in a way that intensifies the aura of Humbert's fixation. Sex itself is lightly evoked: the intimacy between Humbert and Lolita is established in the credit sequence when we see his hands inserting bits of cotton between her toes and painting her toenails; we learn that Humbert and Lolita's mother (Shelley Winters) have become lovers when she wakes up alone in bed and paws the empty space beside her. Nabokov's screenplay is peppered with beguiling double entendres, as when someone refers to Lolita having a cavity filled (instead of a tooth, we immediately think of another cavity), and Humbert's frustration in failing to control Lolita is poignant as well as comic—when the spectacle of pedophilia could have been very disturbing on film. Yet as Humbert tries to assert an adult's sovereignty and Lolita smoothly deflects it, we're able to sympathize with the forlorn figure who is destined for defeat.

Some complained that the fourteen-year-old Sue Lyon looked too mature for her part; while she did emerge as a knowing teenager rather than a child, her mercurial brattishness seemed right for Nabokov's nymphet. But few that I knew shared my enthusiasm for *Lolita* then, because some still had the Fifties' habit of judging films in literary terms; since they regarded the novel as a classic, the movie had to be inferior, even a betrayal of the original. A few were also distressed that Nabokov had stooped to writing the script—not a task for an artist. Nabokov's four-hundred-page screenplay was much longer than the filmed version; he estimated that Kubrick had used about twenty percent of what he wrote, which included material that he had deleted from the book. Even so, Nabokov persistently praised the movie, and he paid tribute to the complexities of adapting fiction or prose for the screen.

Yet where Kubrick had veered from the text, the film was enhanced—especially by Peter Sellers at his best, ranging from the bravado of a casual slob in danger for his life to the languid hauteur of a sham-intellectual, or whisking through a series of disguises. And, unlike most American films of the two preceding decades, *Lolita*'s playful, delicate ghoulishness made dying funny, as when Humbert's exasperating wife was suddenly hit by a car and we knew that he was inwardly delighted. While farces like *Arsenic and Old Lace* had cantered over some parallel territory, the characters weren't racked by the demands of powerful emotions, as Nabokov's and Kubrick's were.

Laughing at death was a novel experience for American audiences. When Kubrick's *Dr. Strangelove, or: How I Learned to Stop Worrying and Love the Bomb* was released in January 1964, many were captivated by a movie that wiped out the world's population—while ridiculing anti-Communists and the Soviet hierarchy and the inadequacies of our presidency and the lunacies of our military establishment. We laughed not only at the gleefully phallic imagery, but because the fanatics continued to function as though they were not about to die: faced with extinction, few of them had the wit to worry. The characters are part of our iconography now: Sterling Hayden as the crazed General Jack D. Ripper, Peter Sellers as the amiable, ineffective President and the rational RAF officer, George C. Scott as the bellicose General Turgidson, Keenan Wynn as the sexually paranoid sergeant, and Slim Pickens as the euphoric bomber—today, most are nearly as familiar as the comic book villains or the trolls and witches of childhood. Although Sellers overplayed the title role, the demented totalitarian has endured as our emblem of a warmaker, and Dr. Strangelove foreshadowed many citizens' perceptions of Henry Kissinger. But while the personae were intricate caricatures, part of Kubrick's strength in *Lolita* and *Dr. Strangelove* resided in understatement, in his low-key approach to Humbert's passion or nuclear holocaust. And *Dr. Strangelove* was paradoxically cheering, because the question of total annihilation could be raised in a medium that had long been so inhibited. While the film's style overturned all the orthodoxies, there was not a hint of preaching.

Sermonizing had been a characteristic of the liberal films of the Fifties; the odor of sanctity had weakened Stanley Kramer's 1959 nuclear movie, *On the Beach,* and most of the well-intended movies about racism or injustice contained some speeches that sounded like homilies. The liberal movies, with few exceptions, had also displayed an uneasiness with the very problems they raised: anti-Semitism or white supremacy weren't seen as endemic to our society, the persecuted librarian in *Storm Center* was a liberal, not a Communist, the boy who was called effeminate in *Tea and Sympathy* was not a homosexual.

Movies that tackled and then sidestepped such issues seemed to mirror the fears that filtered through our national membranes; perhaps the producers thought that racial hatred or sexual uncertainty would be too upsetting for a mass market audience, which might be curious about a "new" or "controversial" subject but would recoil if the material landed too close to home. (Although the theater was more adventurous than Hollywood, I remember that when *West Side Story* opened on Broadway in 1957, there were some shocked reactions to a musical based on warring street gangs; a movie actor told me that it was like setting venereal disease to music.) But *Dr. Strangelove* confronted the most frightening topic of all, and its tone and theme prefigured what was to come: a rebellion against total or unnecessary war throughout a country where military excess and homebaked morality and domestic anti-Communism seemed to lose their legitimacy—at least, for a while.

After radioactive clouds enveloped the world at the end of *Dr. Strangelove,* one could leave the theater with the echo of Vera Lynn singing "We'll meet again, don't know where, don't know when" reverberating in one's ears, oddly elated by a sense of possibility: a movie that defied the traditions of taste and subverted our institutions implied that the Fifties were finally fading. The concept of change had seemed remote to many of us who had grown up with the Cold War: accepting the norm had been the rondo theme of our education, and the future was expected to perpetuate the past. But parts of our culture were beginning to signal that passivity or stoicism need not be quintessential to the national character, and a film like *Dr. Strangelove* suggested that we owed reverence to no fixed authority—and that authority could even be disputed.

Selected Bibliography

Aaron, Daniel. *Writers on the Left*. New York: Harcourt, Brace & World, 1961.

Agee on Film. New York: Grosset & Dunlap (The Universal Library), 1969.

Aronson, James. *The Press and the Cold War*. Indianapolis: Bobbs-Merrill, 1970.

Baldwin, James. *The Devil Finds Work*. New York: Dial Press, 1976.

Belfrage, Cedric. *The American Inquisition*. Indianapolis: Bobbs-Merrill, 1973.

Bentley, Eric. *Are You Now or Have You Ever Been*. New York: Harper Colophon, 1972.

———, ed. *Thirty Years of Treason*. New York: Viking Press, 1971.

Bessie, Alvah. *Inquisition in Eden*. New York: Macmillan, 1965.

Biberman, Herbert. *Salt of the Earth*. Boston: Beacon Press, 1965.

Blum, John Morton. *V Was for Victory: Politics and Culture During World War II*. New York: Harcourt Brace Jovanovich, 1976.

Bogle, Donald. *Toms, Coons, Mammies, and Bucks*. New York: Viking Press, 1973.

Bosworth, Patricia. *Montgomery Clift*. New York: Harcourt Brace Jovanovich, 1978.

Caute, David. *The Fellow Travellers*. New York: Macmillan, 1973.

———. *The Great Fear*. New York: Simon and Schuster, 1978.

Ceplair, Larry, and Steven Englund. *The Inquisition in Hollywood*. New York: Doubleday (Anchor Press/Doubleday), 1980.

Ciment, Michel. *Kazan on Kazan*. New York: Viking Press, 1974.

Clurman, Harold. *All People Are Famous*. New York: Harcourt Brace Jovanovich, 1974.

———. *The Fervent Years*. New York: Harvest, Harcourt Brace Jovanovich, 1975.

221

Cogley, John. *Report on Blacklisting,* Vol. 1. The Fund for the Republic, 1956.

Committee on Un-American Activities, U.S. 80th Congress, First Session, October 1947. *Hearings Regarding the Communist Infiltration of the Motion Picture Industry.* Washington, D.C.: U.S. Government Printing Office, 1947.

Committee on Un-American Activities, U.S. House of Representatives. *100 Things You Should Know About COMMUNISM.* Washington, D.C.: U.S. Government Printing Office, 1951.

Cook, Bruce. *Dalton Trumbo.* New York: Charles Scribner's Sons. 1977.

Cowley, Malcolm. *The Dream of the Golden Mountains: Remembering the Thirties.* New York: Viking Press, 1980.

————. *And I Worked at the Writer's Trade.* New York: Viking Press, 1978.

Crowther, Bosley. *Hollywood Rajah: The Life and Times of Louis B. Mayer.* New York: Henry Holt, 1960.

Davies, Joseph. *Mission to Moscow.* New York: Charles Scribner's Sons, 1941.

De Mille, Cecil B. *The Autobiography of Cecil B. De Mille.* New York: Prentice-Hall, 1959.

Dies, Martin. *The Trojan Horse in America.* New York: Dodd, Mead, 1940.

Donner, Frank. *The Un-Americans.* New York: Ballantine Books, 1961.

Dowdy, Andrew. *The Films of the Fifties.* New York: Morrow, 1973.

Dunne, Philip. *Take Two.* New York: McGraw-Hill, 1980.

Farber, Manny. *Movies.* New York: Hillstone, 1971.

Garfield, David. *A Player's Place: The Story of the Actors Studio.* New York: Macmillan, 1980.

Garnham, Nicholas. *Samuel Fuller.* New York: Viking Press, 1971.

Goodman, Walter. *The Committee.* New York: Farrar, Straus & Giroux, 1968.

Gow, Gordon. *Hollywood in the Fifties.* New York: A. S. Barnes, 1971.

Graham Greene on Film: Collected Film Criticism 1935–1939. New York: Simon and Schuster, 1972.

Gussow, Mel. *Don't Say Yes Until I Finish Talking: A Biography of Darryl F. Zanuck.* New York: Pocket Books, 1972.

Haskell, Molly. *From Reverence to Rape.* New York: Holt, Rinehart and Winston, 1973.

Hayden, Sterling. *Wanderer.* New York: Knopf, 1963.

Hellman, Lillian. *Scoundrel Time*. Boston: Little, Brown, 1976.

Kanfer, Stefan. *A Journal of the Plague Years*. New York: Atheneum, 1973.

Kempton, Murray. *America Comes of Middle Age*. Boston: Little, Brown, 1963.

————. *Part of Our Time*. New York: Dell (Delta Books), 1967.

Kennan, George F. *Memoirs: 1925–1950*. Boston: Little, Brown, 1967.

Knightley, Phillip. *The First Casualty*. New York: Harcourt Brace Jovanovich, 1975.

Koch, Howard. *As Time Goes By*. New York: Harcourt Brace Jovanovich, 1979.

Koury, Phil. *Yes, Mr. De Mille*. New York: G. P. Putnam's Sons, 1959.

Kraft, Hy. *On My Way to the Theater*. New York: Macmillan, 1971.

Lardner, Ring, Jr. *The Lardners: My Family Remembered*. New York: Harper & Row (Colophon), 1977.

Lasch, Christopher. *The New Radicalism in America: 1889–1963*. New York: Knopf, 1965.

Martin, John Barlow. *Adlai Stevenson of Illinois*. New York: Doubleday (Anchor Books), 1977.

Marx, Arthur. *Goldwyn*. New York: W. W. Norton, 1976.

Marx, Samuel. *Mayer and Thalberg: The Make-Believe Saints*. New York: Random House, 1975.

MacCann, Richard Dyer. *The People's Films*. New York: Hastings House, 1973.

McWilliams, Carey. *The Education of Carey McWilliams*. New York: Simon and Schuster, 1979.

————. *Witch Hunt*. Boston: Little, Brown, 1950.

Miller, Arthur. *After the Fall*. New York: Bantam Books, 1965.

————. *The Crucible*. New York: Viking Press, 1953.

————. *The Theater Essays of Arthur Miller*. New York: Viking Press, 1978.

————. *A View from the Bridge*. New York: Viking Press, 1955.

Miller, Douglas T., and Marion Nowak. *The Fifties*. New York: Doubleday, 1977.

Mitford, Jessica. *A Fine Old Conflict*. New York: Knopf, 1977.

Navasky, Victor. *Naming Names*. New York: Viking Press, 1980.

Pells, Richard H. *Radical Visions and American Dreams*. New York: Harper & Row, 1973.

Phillips, Gene D. *Stanley Kubrick: A Film Odyssey*. New York: Popular Library, 1977.

Powdermaker, Hortense. *Hollywood: The Dream Factory.* Boston: Little, Brown, 1950.

Rovere, Richard H. *Senator Joe McCarthy.* New York: Harcourt, Brace & World, 1959.

Schary, Dore. *Heyday.* Boston: Little, Brown, 1979.

Sklar, Robert. *Movie-Made America.* New York: Random House, 1975.

Stanley, Robert. *The Celluloid Empire.* New York: Hastings House, 1978.

Stewart, Donald Ogden. *By a Stroke of Luck!* New York: Paddington Press, 1975.

Stone, I. F. *The Haunted Fifties.* New York: Random House, 1963.

Swanberg, W. A. *Luce and His Empire.* New York: Dell, 1973.

Talbot, David, and Barbara Zheutlin. *Creative Differences.* Boston: South End Press, 1978.

Thomas, Bob. *King Cohn.* New York: G. P. Putnam's Sons, 1967.

Truffaut, François. *The Films in My Life.* New York: Simon and Schuster, 1975.

Trumbo, Dalton. *Additional Dialogue: The Letters of Dalton Trumbo.* New York: M. Evans, 1970.

Vaughn, Robert. *Only Victims.* New York: G. P. Putnam's Sons, 1972.

Viertel, Salka. *The Kindness of Strangers.* New York: Holt, Rinehart and Winston, 1969.

Warner, Jack. *My First Hundred Years in Hollywood.* New York: Random House, 1965.

Williams, Robert C. *Russian Art and American Money.* Cambridge: Harvard University Press, 1980.

Yergin, Daniel. *The Shattered Peace.* Boston: Houghton Mifflin, 1977.

PERIODICALS

Brandon, Henry. "Interview with Arthur Miller." *Harper's Magazine,* November 1960.

Cvetic, Matthew (as told to Pete Martin). "I Posed as a Communist for the FBI." *The Saturday Evening Post,* July 15, 22, and 29, 1950.

Film Culture. ed. Gordon Hitchens, Fall and Winter 1970.

Films in Review, "Salt of the Earth." April 1954.

Kazan, Elia. "Letters to the Editor." *Saturday Review,* April 15, 1952.

Lardner, Ring, Jr. "My Life on the Blacklist." *The Saturday Evening Post*, October 14, 1961.

Miller, Arthur. "The Year It Came Apart." *New York* magazine, December 30, 1974.

O'Reilly, Kenneth. "The FBI—HUAC's Big Brother." *The Nation*, January 19, 1980.

Ross, Lillian. "Onward and Upward with the Arts: Come In, Lassie!" *The New Yorker*, February 21, 1948.

Taradash, Daniel. "Storm Center Course." *The New York Times*, October 14, 1956.

Screen Credits

CHAPTER I

Crossfire: directed by Edward Dmytryk, screenplay by John Paxton, produced by Adrian Scott, 1947.

Gentleman's Agreement: directed by Elia Kazan, screenplay by Moss Hart, produced by Darryl F. Zanuck, 1947.

Pinky: directed by Elia Kazan, screenplay by Philip Dunne and Dudley Nichols, produced by Darryl F. Zanuck, 1949.

Home of the Brave: directed by Mark Robson, screenplay by Carl Foreman, produced by Stanley Kramer, 1949.

Intruder in the Dust: directed by Clarence Brown, screenplay by Ben Maddow, produced by Clarence Brown, 1949.

No Way Out: directed by Joseph Mankiewicz, screenplay by Joseph Mankiewicz and Lesser Samuels, produced by Darryl F. Zanuck, 1950.

The Best Years of Our Lives: directed by William Wyler, screenplay by Robert E. Sherwood, produced by Samuel Goldwyn, 1946.

The Senator Was Indiscreet: directed by George Kaufman, screenplay by Charles MacArthur and Nunnally Johnson, produced by Nunnally Johnson, 1947.

CHAPTER II

Mission to Moscow: directed by Michael Curtiz, screenplay by Howard Koch, produced by Robert Buckner, 1943.

Song of Russia: directed by Gregory Ratoff, screenplay by Paul Jarrico and Richard Collins, produced by Joseph Pasternak, 1944.

Tender Comrade: directed by Edward Dmytryk, screenplay by Dalton Trumbo, produced by David Hempstead, 1944.

The Fountainhead: directed by King Vidor, screenplay by Ayn **Rand,** produced by Henry Blanke, 1949.

CHAPTER III

The Red Menace: directed by R. G. Springsteen, screenplay by Albert DeMond and Gerald Geraghty, 1949.

I Was a Communist for the FBI: directed by Gordon Douglas, screenplay by Crane Wilbur, produced by Bryan Foy, 1951.

Walk East on Beacon: directed by Alfred Werker, screenplay by Leo Rosten, produced by Louis de Rochemont, 1952.

My Son John: directed by Leo McCarey, screenplay by Myles Connolly and Leo McCarey, produced by Leo McCarey, 1952.

CHAPTER IV

East of Eden: directed by Elia Kazan, screenplay by Paul Osborn, produced by Elia Kazan, 1955.

Rebel Without a Cause: directed by Nicholas Ray, screenplay by Stewart Stern, produced by David Weisbart, 1955.

The Wild Party: directed by Harry Horner, screenplay by John McPartland, produced by Sidney Harmon, 1956.

The Blackboard Jungle: directed by Richard Brooks, screenplay by Richard Brooks, produced by Pandro S. Berman, 1955.

The Man with the Golden Arm: directed by Otto Preminger, screenplay by Walter Newman and Lewis Meltzer, produced by Otto Preminger, 1955.

A Hatful of Rain: directed by Fred Zinnemann, screenplay by Michael V. Gazzo and Alfred Hayes, produced by Buddy Adler, 1957.

A Place in the Sun: directed by George Stevens, screenplay by Michael Wilson and Harry Brown, produced by George Stevens, 1951.

From Here to Eternity: directed by Fred Zinnemann, screenplay by Daniel Taradash, produced by Buddy Adler, 1953.

Executive Suite: directed by Robert Wise, screenplay by Ernest Lehman, produced by John Houseman, 1954.

The Man in the Gray Flannel Suit: directed by Nunnally Johnson, screenplay by Nunnally Johnson, produced by Darryl F. Zanuck, 1956.

Patterns: directed by Fielder Cook, screenplay by Rod Serling, produced by Michael Myerberg, 1956.

All About Eve: directed by Joseph Mankiewicz, written by Joseph Mankiewicz, produced by Darryl F. Zanuck, 1950.

Compulsion: directed by Richard Fleischer, screenplay by Richard Murphy, produced by Richard D. Zanuck, 1959.

Tea and Sympathy: directed by Vincente Minnelli, screenplay by Robert Anderson, produced by Pandro S. Berman, 1956.

CHAPTER V

On the Waterfront: directed by Elia Kazan, screenplay by Budd Schulberg, produced by Sam Spiegel, 1954.

A Face in the Crowd: directed by Elia Kazan, screenplay by Budd Schulberg, produced by Elia Kazan, 1957.

CHAPTER VI

Salt of the Earth: directed by Herbert Biberman, screenplay by Michael Wilson, produced by Paul Jarrico, 1954.

High Noon: directed by Fred Zinnemann, screenplay by Carl Foreman, produced by Stanley Kramer, 1952.

Storm Center: directed by Daniel Taradash, screenplay by Daniel Taradash and Elick Moll, produced by Julian Blaustein, 1956.

Twelve Angry Men: directed by Sidney Lumet, screenplay by Reginald Rose, produced by Henry Fonda and Reginald Rose, 1957.

Edge of the City: directed by Martin Ritt, screenplay by Robert Alan Aurthur, produced by David Susskind, 1957.

The Defiant Ones: directed by Stanley Kramer, screenplay by Nedrick Young and Harold Jacob Smith, produced by Stanley Kramer, 1958.

The Steel Helmet: directed by Samuel Fuller, screenplay by Samuel Fuller, produced by Samuel Fuller, 1951.

The Bridge on the River Kwai: directed by David Lean, screenplay by Carl Foreman and Michael Wilson, produced by Sam Spiegel, 1957.

Paths of Glory: directed by Stanley Kubrick, screenplay by Stanley Kubrick, Calder Willingham, and Jim Thompson, produced by James B. Harris, 1957.

CHAPTER VII

Them!: directed by Gordon Douglas, screenplay by Ted Sherdeman, produced by David Weisbart, 1954.

The Day the Earth Stood Still: directed by Robert Wise, screenplay by Edmund H. North, produced by Julian Blaustein, 1951.

The Blob: directed by Irvin S. Yeaworth, Jr., screenplay by Irving H. Millgate, produced by Jack H. Harris, 1958.

The Thing: directed by Christian Nyby, screenplay by Charles Lederer, produced by Howard Hawks, 1951.

Invaders from Mars: directed by William Cameron Menzies, screenplay by Richard Blake, produced by Edward L. Alperson, 1953.

Invasion of the Body Snatchers: directed by Don Siegel, screenplay by Daniel Mainwaring, produced by Walter Wanger, 1956.

The Next Voice You Hear . . . : directed by William Wellman, screenplay by Charles Schnee, produced by Dore Schary, 1950.

Red Planet Mars: directed by Harry Horner, screenplay by John L. Balderston and Anthony Veiller, produced by Anthony Veiller, 1952.

The Ten Commandments: directed by Cecil B. De Mille, screenplay by Aeneas Mackenzie, Jesse L. Lasky, Jr., Jack Gariss, and Frederic M. Frank, produced by Cecil B. De Mille, 1956.

Lolita: directed by Stanley Kubrick, screenplay by Vladimir Nabokov, produced by James B. Harris, 1962.

Dr. Strangelove, or: How I Learned to Stop Worrying and Love the Bomb: directed by Stanley Kubrick, screenplay by Stanley Kubrick, Terry Southern, and Peter George, produced by Stanley Kubrick, 1964.

Photo Credits

Force of Evil: National Telefilm Associates, Courtesy of the Museum of Modern Art

Crossfire: RKO, Courtesy of the Museum of Modern Art

Gentleman's Agreement: 20th Century-Fox

Home of the Brave: United Artists, Courtesy of the Museum of Modern Art

Intruder in the Dust: M-G-M, Courtesy of the Museum of Modern Art

No Way Out: 20th Century-Fox, Courtesy of the Museum of Modern Art

The Best Years of Our Lives: Samuel Goldwyn Studios, Courtesy of the Museum of Modern Art

Mission to Moscow: United Artists, Courtesy of the Museum of Modern Art

Mission to Moscow: United Artists

Song of Russia: M-G-M

The North Star: Samuel Goldwyn Studios

Song of Russia: M-G-M

The Fountainhead: United Artists, Courtesy of the Museum of Modern Art

I Married a Communist: RKO, Courtesy of the Museum of Modern Art

I Was a Communist for the FBI: Warner Brothers

Walk East on Beacon: Columbia, Courtesy of the Museum of Modern Art

Trial: M-G-M, Courtesy of the Museum of Modern Art

My Son John: Paramount, Courtesy of the Museum of Modern Art

The Long, Hot Summer: 20th Century-Fox, Courtesy of the Museum of Modern Art

East of Eden: Warner Brothers, Courtesy of the Museum of Modern Art

Red River: United Artists, Courtesy of the Museum of Modern Art

East of Eden: Warner Brothers, Courtesy of the Museum of Modern Art

Ashes and Diamonds: Janus Films

The Wild One: Columbia, Courtesy of the Museum of Modern Art

The Man in the Gray Flannel Suit: 20th Century-Fox, Courtesy of the Museum of Modern Art

The Blackboard Jungle: M-G-M, Courtesy of the Museum of Modern Art

The Catered Affair: M-G-M, Courtesy of the Museum of Modern Art

No Down Payment: 20th Century-Fox, Courtesy of the Museum of Modern Art

The Apartment: United Artists

231

The Swan: M-G-M, Courtesy of the Museum of Modern Art
Sabrina: Paramount, Courtesy of the Museum of Modern Art
Patterns: United Artists
All About Eve: 20th Century-Fox, Courtesy of the Museum of Modern Art
Tea and Sympathy: M-G-M, Courtesy of the Museum of Modern Art
On the Waterfront: Columbia, Courtesy of the Museum of Modern Art
On the Waterfront: Columbia, Courtesy of the Museum of Modern Art
On the Waterfront: Columbia, Courtesy of the Museum of Modern Art
Baby Doll: Newtown Productions
A Face in the Crowd: Newtown Productions, Courtesy of the Museum of Modern Art
High Noon: National Telefilm Associates, Courtesy of the Museum of Modern Art
Storm Center: Columbia
The Steel Helmet: Deputy Corporation, Courtesy of the Museum of Modern Art
The Bridge on the River Kwai: Columbia, Courtesy of the Museum of Modern Art
Paths of Glory: United Artists
Them!: Warner Brothers, Courtesy of the Museum of Modern Art
The Day the Earth Stood Still: 20th Century-Fox
Invaders from Mars: 20th Century-Fox
Invasion of the Body Snatchers: Lorimar Productions, Inc.
Invaders from Mars: 20th Century-Fox
Samson and Delilah: Paramount, Courtesy of the Museum of Modern Art
The Robe: 20th Century-Fox, Courtesy of the Museum of Modern Art
The Ten Commandments: Paramount, Courtesy of the Museum of Modern Art

Index